Young Scholars Model

Young Scholars Model

A Comprehensive Approach for Developing Talent and Pursuing Equity in Gifted Education

Carol V. Horn, Ed.D., Catherine A. Little, Ph.D., Kirsten Maloney, & Cheryl McCullough

PRUFROCK PRESS INC.™

PRUFROCK ACADEMIC PRESS

A line of materials supporting scholarship and research-based practices in education

Library of Congress Cataloging-in-Publication Data

Names: Horn, Carol V., 1949- author.
Title: Young Scholars Model : a comprehensive approach for developing
   talent and pursuing equity in gifted education / Carol V. Horn,
   Catherine Anne Little, Kirsten Novak Maloney, Cheryl Ann McCullough.
Description: Waco,TX : Prufrock Press Inc., 2021. | Includes
   bibliographical references. | Summary: "Historically, students from
   ethnically, linguistically, and economically diverse backgrounds have
   been overlooked and underidentified for gifted services"-- Provided by
   publisher.
Identifiers: LCCN 2021011334 (print) | LCCN 2021011335 (ebook) | ISBN
   9781646321254 (paperback) | ISBN 9781646321261 (ebook) | ISBN
   9781646321278 (epub)
Subjects: LCSH: Gifted children--Education--Social aspects--United States.
   | Gifted children--United States--Social conditions. | Children with
   social disabilities--Education--United States.
Classification: LCC LC3993.9 .H67 2021 (print) | LCC LC3993.9 (ebook) |
   DDC 371.95--dc23
LC record available at https://lccn.loc.gov/2021011334
LC ebook record available at https://lccn.loc.gov/2021011335

Edited by Stephanie McCauley

Cover design and layout design by Shelby Charette

ISBN-13: 978-1-64632-125-4

Printed in the United States of America.

At the time of this book's publication, all facts and figures cited are the most current available. All telephone numbers, addresses, and website URLs are accurate and active. All publications, organizations, websites, and other resources exist as described in the book, and all have been verified. The authors and Prufrock Press Inc. make no warranty or guarantee concerning the information and materials given out by organizations or content found at websites, and we are not responsible for any changes that occur after this book's publication. If you find an error, please contact Prufrock Press Inc.

Prufrock Press Inc.
P.O. Box 8813
Waco, TX 76714-8813
Phone: (800) 998-2208
Fax: (800) 240-0333
https://www.prufrock.com

Dedication

We dedicate this book to all of the young scholars,
school teams, and families who have made the vision of
the Young Scholars Model a powerful reality.

Table of Contents

Acknowledgments   ix

Foreword   xi

Introduction   1

CHAPTER 1 | Background and Overview of the
                 Young Scholars Model   3

CHAPTER 2 | School and District Leadership   21

CHAPTER 3 | Seeking and Identifying Potential
                 in Young Scholars   47

CHAPTER 4 | High-Quality Curriculum   71

CHAPTER 5 | Professional Learning   97

CHAPTER 6 | Partnering With Families   119

CHAPTER 7 | Enrichment Opportunities   133

CHAPTER 8 | Expanding the Young Scholars Model
                 to Other Schools and Districts   153

References   183

Appendix: Sample Applications of Critical and Creative
Thinking Strategies   191

About the Authors   209

Table of Contents

Acknowledgments

We want to thank the many educators and students who contributed their stories to this text—your voices made the model come alive. We thank all of the central office teams and school teams we have worked with to support and encourage students and those who work with them. We acknowledge also the leadership of scholars and practitioners in the field of gifted education who have worked tirelessly to advance the goals of equity and excellence.

Special thanks to Rachael Cody for research assistance and Addicus Bagwell for his graphic design work on the icons throughout the book.

Foreword

I am so pleased to see this book on the Young Scholars Model come to fruition. I encouraged Carol Horn and her colleagues to write about their work so that others may benefit from their insights and experience gained over many years. I am a stalwart fan of the model, as it illustrates and incorporates so many best practices to ensure more equitable identification of giftedness and talent. It fits squarely with a talent development framework for gifted education services. The many best practices that the model incorporates are:

- Early intervention because the research shows that students from lower income families start school already behind in achievement compared to their more advantaged peers.
- Training teachers to provide challenging instruction to *all* learners because challenging work enables students to demonstrate higher level thinking, problem-solving skills, and persistence that might otherwise go unnoticed.
- Collaboration between gifted specialists and classroom teachers, thereby reinforcing the importance of a school-wide commitment to discovering talent.

- The use of multiple tools and local norms to identify high potential with the goal of providing opportunities that enable students to qualify for future services that use district-level norms.
- The use of outside-of-school time to provide additional instruction and enrichment, thereby leveling the playing field in terms of opportunity gaps.
- A well-defined, articulated, shared outcome for gifted programming: identifying and preparing more students to evidence their talent in advanced achievement and get onto talent development trajectories.
- Reversing the typical approach to gifted education of "assessment followed by services" to "services followed by assessment," with significant front-loading of opportunities.
- The provision of continuous pathways across grades K–12, with multiple entry points and on-ramps, consistent with research about the importance of talent development trajectories.
- Training teachers to be talent scouts who make recommendations based on students' performances in authentic contexts.
- Intentional school leadership focused on equity, inclusion, diversity, and talent development.
- A focus, within programming and opportunities, to develop and actively cultivate mindsets and other psychosocial skills that support talent development.
- A schoolwide model that includes the features just outlined but also latitude and encouragement to customize based on the uniqueness of the school context and student population.
- A districtwide model that includes different types of gifted services for students at different stages of talent development rather than gifted programs.

The Young Scholars Model has a proven track record of success demonstrated by increases in the diversity of the students identified and the numbers of students who are prepared to progress to higher, more selective, and rigorous talent development opportunities. The model has been replicated in many districts throughout the United States and has been an influential force for change and equity within the field of gifted education. Additionally, the work of these writers/practitioners has shown how a talent development framework benefits students of all abilities and the entire school.

The Young Scholars Model came about in response to the problem of lack of socioeconomic, cultural, and linguistic diversity within gifted programs. It was not designed as a methodologically rigorous research study. The model was refined over time as experience and learning revealed what did and did not work. The Young Scholars Model is a testament to the efficacy of school-based educators in designing innovative and successful approaches to the most vexing problems within our education system—achievement, excellence, and opportunity gaps. It is my hope that this book will help other educators to feel empowered to do the same.

—Paula Olszewski-Kubilius, Ph.D., Director of the Center for
Talent Development at Northwestern University

Introduction

Since the inception of programs and services for gifted learners, certain populations of students have been denied access to gifted services and the advanced learning opportunities that such programs provide. Children who are different because of their race, socioeconomic level, or primary language have been discounted and overlooked, and historically very few efforts were made to remedy the situation. Test scores, biased assessments, and limited teacher referrals are just a few of the reasons children from diverse backgrounds rarely qualified for advanced academic programs and services.

The Young Scholars Model (sometimes referred to simply as "Young Scholars") is a comprehensive, schoolwide effort to address this issue. In schools that have adopted the model, administrators and teachers play a major role in addressing the inequities that have plagued our society for too long. They realize that the structures of our school system place educators in a unique position to cross cultural, ethnic, socioeconomic, and linguistic boundaries to provide all students equal access to gifted services. They find that when high expectations for all students are supported with best practices to reach those expectations, the entire school community values and advocates for each and every child who comes through the door.

The Young Scholars Model builds capacity in schools to embrace a new way of thinking about gifted/advanced academic potential in students. It requires a shift from an understanding of intelligence as a static and innate ability grounded in a cultural and social context tied to Western, affluent, mostly White populations to an understanding of intelligence as emerging potential, evolving over time, in response to and mediated by external and internal catalysts. This new way of thinking supports the need to find and develop talent in a much broader range of students. These expanded beliefs require culturally responsive measures of a child's ability to think, reason, and problem solve. Schools that make a concerted effort to value the differences that children bring to school and to provide multiple opportunities for students to demonstrate and develop their academic strengths ensure access to advanced academic services for all populations.

This book describes the major components of the Young Scholars Model and how they interact in efforts to find and nurture potential in students who have historically been overlooked for gifted services. We also outline steps for implementation and guidelines for monitoring and evaluation so that school districts will be able to replicate the model with fidelity and success. The model consists of focused attention to the following elements:

- ≈ collaborative leadership;
- ≈ nontraditional methods of finding, nurturing, and developing talent;
- ≈ high-quality curriculum and instruction;
- ≈ professional learning;
- ≈ parent and family partnerships; and
- ≈ enrichment opportunities.

This is a dynamic, comprehensive approach to the issue of underrepresentation that ensures that all students have access to advanced learning opportunities that build on their strengths so that they may achieve their highest potential.

Chapter 1

Background and Overview of the Young Scholars Model

If you treat an individual as he is, he will remain how he is.
But if you treat him as if he were what he ought to be and
could be, he will become what he ought to be and could be.
—Johann Wolfgang von Goethe

The Young Scholars Model is grounded in a belief system that necessitates a major paradigm shift in the notion of giftedness. The following statements capture the core beliefs that underlie the foundation of the model. Each chapter begins with a set of beliefs that elaborate on these statements and that underlie the work of the educators engaged in implementing the model.

We believe . . .

- ✦ Exceptional talent and academic ability exist in all populations.
- ✦ Implementation of the Young Scholars Model requires a community of professionals working together with a shared commitment to find and develop talent in all children.
- ✦ Ongoing assessment by educators who have been trained to provide curriculum and instruction that are designed to elicit gifted behaviors may be the most powerful means of finding and nurturing gifted learners from underrepresented populations.
- ✦ High-level curriculum and instruction infused with gifted education pedagogy are an integral part of both finding and nurturing advanced potential in students from historically underrepresented groups.
- ✦ Ongoing professional learning efforts on multiple levels (i.e., district leaders, school administrators, and school staff) are critical to the success of the model. These include a focus on talent development, cultural proficiency, performance assessments, and the development of a growth mindset.
- ✦ Providing access to accelerated programs and enrichment resources is crucial for students who may not otherwise have access due to financial constraints or other obstacles beyond their control. Such programs and resources may include summer school, afterschool activities, field trips, and/or weekend programs through the school district or university partnerships.
- ✦ Building parent partnerships and family relationships is essential. Schools that implement the Young Scholars Model actively work to strengthen parent and family connections.

In this chapter . . .

- ✦ We explain the rationale for the Young Scholars Model.
- ✦ We share the historical context in which the model evolved.
- ✦ We outline the goals and major components of the model.
- ✦ We share voices from the field of educators and students who have had direct experience with the model.

Rationale for the Model

The underrepresentation of students from culturally, economically, and linguistically diverse backgrounds in gifted and talented programs across the United States is one of the most critical equity problems facing public educators today (Peters et al., 2019; Wells, 2020). Underrepresentation means that learners are denied access to learning experiences that are appropriately challenging for their needs, and that their long-term opportunities for accessing advanced learning are limited as well. Research suggests that students from diverse cultural, linguistic, and economic backgrounds tend to be identified for gifted programs and advanced learning opportunities at rates lower than their peers at the elementary level (Olszewski-Kubilius & Corwith, 2018). There are many contributing factors, including limited or inconsistent teacher referrals, an overemphasis on test scores, and/or low expectations (Ford, 2010; Peters et al., 2019). Consequently, as they progress through school, they continue to be underrepresented in honors classes, Advanced Placement (AP) courses, accelerated learning, and higher education opportunities (Hodges et al., 2018). These are components and contributing factors to the *excellence gap*, which is the term for the disparity between demographic groups in advanced levels of performance in education (Plucker & Peters, 2016).

In response to the ongoing underrepresentation of students from diverse groups in advanced learning programs, two major questions must be addressed, centering on the concepts of equity and excellence:

- How do educators ensure that every student with gifted potential has equal access to gifted services and advanced academic opportunities?
- How can gifted programs be more inclusive without compromising high standards?

On the issue of equity, some might dismiss all programs for the gifted as being elitist and serving the needs of only a privileged few. Others would advocate for excellence, believing that students with high ability need gifted services to progress at a rate that is commensurate with their advanced capacity to think, reason, and learn. Through our work and research we have discovered that there are many more students who are able to participate and succeed in curricular experiences that were once reserved for a small identified group of gifted learners. We have also learned that by using curriculum and instruction that is research-based and specifically designed for gifted learners, teachers are able to include more students while maintaining high standards.

Although research suggests that biased identification procedures (e.g., a reliance on tests that require verbal and mathematical proficiency) and/or limited teacher referrals are major causes of the underrepresentation of gifted learners from diverse cultural, linguistic, and economic backgrounds (Bernal, 2002; Castellano & Díaz, 2001), there is a dearth of viable solutions and programs documenting recommendations and actions that may be taken to remedy the situation (Donovan & Cross, 2002; Hodges et al., 2018).

Studies have shown that students from underrepresented populations who have the potential to succeed in advanced academic programs but never gain access are more likely to drop out of school and less likely to pursue higher education (Ford et al., 2002; Scott et al., 1996). For students from traditionally underserved cultural, socioeconomic, and linguistic backgrounds, low teacher expectations and academic labeling that may narrow their options often affect the goals that they set for themselves and lead to disengagement from school. These students often receive more of a rote learning and skills-based approach that does little or nothing to develop their exceptional potential (Olszewski-Kubilius & Thomson, 2010; Smith et al., 1997). Teachers may view students from diverse backgrounds as unable or unwilling to engage in higher level thinking and may even have concerns that these students will hold back the high achievers if placed in the same classrooms (Olszewski-Kubilius & Corwith, 2018).

Many studies focus on the struggles or perceived deficits of children from underrepresented populations rather than on areas of strength that can be nurtured and developed (Ford et al., 2002; Plucker et al., 2010). Traditionally the label "underachiever" is given to a student who achieves high scores on standardized tests but does not perform well in school. However, according to Ford (2010), there is another population of underachievers who have never had an *opportunity* to achieve at a high level. These are the students from diverse backgrounds who may score poorly on standardized ability tests and yet have the capacity to perform at a high level if given the opportunity. For these students, low achievement becomes a self-fulfilling prophecy that must be changed in two directions. Not only must teachers believe that the students can work at a high level, but also the students must believe they can do the work; such belief emerges through participation in educational experiences designed to challenge their minds and expand their horizons (Ford, 2010; Ford et al., 2002). Further, it is important for these kinds of interventions to begin early in the school years and to be sustained across time to prevent relative slowing of learning rates for some populations of learners as they progress (Rambo-Hernandez et al., 2019).

Although there are many recommendations around the need to address the underrepresentation of students from diverse backgrounds in gifted education programs, few studies evaluate significant efforts, recommendations, and/or programs that are being implemented to solve this problem (Donovan & Cross, 2002; Ford, 2010).

Origins of the Young Scholars Model

A growing concern with the continuous underrepresentation of Black and Hispanic students, students from backgrounds of poverty, and English language learners (ELLs) in gifted programs led the gifted and talented central office staff in a large east coast school district to take a more comprehensive approach to this issue during the 1999–2000 school year. Previous changes and initiatives to address the problem of underrepresentation tended to focus on identification criteria and the use of multiple forms of data to make decisions. However, these changes did little to increase the participation of underrepresented populations in the gifted and talented programs.

The district's central office staff decided to create a task force of principals and teachers at schools with high numbers of students from diverse cultural, socioeconomic, and linguistic backgrounds. The task force was charged with finding ways to rethink current practice and to design a comprehensive approach to the issue of underrepresentation. Through reading, research, and conversations the task force determined that attention to identification alone was not enough. The students needed early interventions and access to learning opportunities that developed and elicited higher level thinking, all of which would prepare them for success in advanced coursework. They also needed teachers who believed in their advanced potential and who were willing to advocate for them and nurture their strengths so that their potential would be affirmed and developed.

Working closely with the principals and staff in the identified schools, the task force developed a comprehensive approach to the issue of underrepresentation, which evolved into a model that could be replicated by others. The new model developed by this team of stakeholders was called Young Scholars, and it embraced current thinking and research on best practices for finding and nurturing gifted potential in all populations.

The Young Scholars Model (Figure 1) was initially piloted in 12 schools that had diverse student populations overall but very little diversity in the students who were participating in gifted services. Under the leadership of the school principals, teachers and educational specialists worked together to identify students with gifted potential in kindergarten through grade 2 as young scholars. They used classroom observations, anecdotal records, and portfolios of student work.

Figure 1
The Young Scholars Model

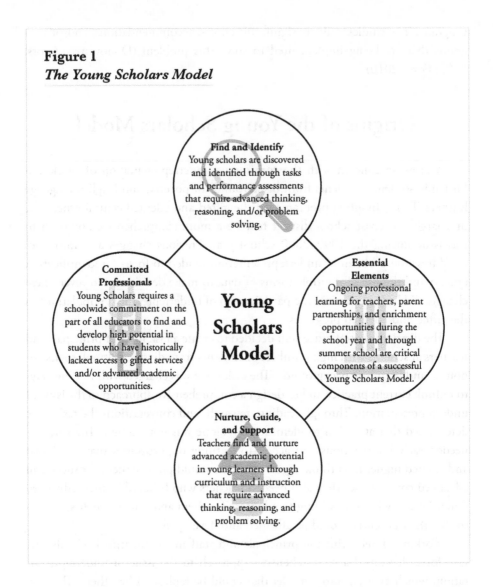

Find and Identify
Young scholars are discovered and identified through tasks and performance assessments that require advanced thinking, reasoning, and/or problem solving.

Committed Professionals
Young Scholars requires a schoolwide commitment on the part of all educators to find and develop high potential in students who have historically lacked access to gifted services and/or advanced academic opportunities.

Young Scholars Model

Essential Elements
Ongoing professional learning for teachers, parent partnerships, and enrichment opportunities during the school year and through summer school are critical components of a successful Young Scholars Model.

Nurture, Guide, and Support
Teachers find and nurture advanced academic potential in young learners through curriculum and instruction that require advanced thinking, reasoning, and problem solving.

As students were identified, the team offered them learning opportunities that included summer school and afterschool activities. These were accompanied by professional learning opportunities for the teachers and educational offerings for the parents. The goal was to ensure that every child with an exceptional capacity to learn, reason, and apply knowledge was nurtured at an early age and prepared to participate in formal gifted and talented programs and/or advanced academic courses.

Voices From the Field

Growing up in rural Ethiopia, my mother did not receive a formal education. My father fared better and attended school until the eighth grade before dropping out. Although they themselves could not reap the benefits of an education, they knew of its limitless potential. Each year, they applied for a chance to immigrate to the United States to procure an education for their children. That opportunity came and my family moved to America.

When we arrived in Washington, DC, I struggled to adapt to the new culture and language. In second grade, my family was informed that I would be transferring from my base school to a school that had a full-time Advanced Academics Program (AAP). I was able to partake in AAP through the Young Scholars program that selects students from low-income backgrounds to partake in AAP. My first year within the program was arduous because the AAP program was more challenging than my base school. However, by my third year within the program, I was on par with my other peers within the AAP program. By middle school, I had even advanced to the top tier of my cohort. The AAP program gave me a strong foundation for my high school International Baccalaureate (IB) courses in which I excelled. With my success in my courses, and the SAT, I was accepted to seven Ivy League universities (I never applied for the eighth one).

What surprises me the most about [the program I experienced] is its ability to select students with potential. The clamour with gifted and talented programs is that they often select the children of well-connected parents and are not based on meritocracy. My story is the antithesis of that argument. Despite my lack of proficiency in English, the Young Scholars program invested in me because they saw unbridled potential. I can undoubtedly say that without the AAP program, I would not be where I am today. Out of my six siblings, only two have gone on to graduate from college. However, the Young Scholars and AAP program placed me, early on in my life, in a highly nurturing learning environment.

—Yosaph Boku, one of the first young scholars and a recent Harvard graduate

Goals and Components of the Young Scholars Model

The Young Scholars Model has two important goals. The first is to identify talent potential in children from diverse cultural, economic, and linguistic backgrounds as early as possible. The second goal is to nurture, guide, and support the development of the students' exceptional potential. The emphasis is on seeking students who are showing potential that is exceptional (i.e., atypical) compared to peers of similar age, experience, and background, thus indicating that their academic needs may include more advanced learning opportunities. School districts that have implemented the model have experienced systemic change and a dramatic increase in the number of students from diverse populations receiving gifted services.

In Young Scholars schools, all students are exposed to experiences that are designed to elicit behaviors that may indicate high potential. As this potential emerges, the students who are designated as young scholars are clustered in classrooms with teachers who are trained in gifted education pedagogy. The teachers collaborate, plan, design, and implement learning experiences that connect to the students' diverse cultural, economic, and linguistic backgrounds. Basic skills are strengthened through lessons that also require students to think and apply knowledge on a higher, more complex level.

It is important to note that, from the beginning, young scholars are held to the same high standards and performance expectations as other advanced learners. The main difference is in the scaffolding and support that is provided to promote and nurture their advanced academic ability. The long-term goal is to find students with high academic potential from historically underrepresented populations at an early age, raise their personal expectations, support family involvement, and prepare them for participation in advanced academic opportunities as they advance in grade level.

Four Major Components

The model has four major components that together support the efforts to search for and nurture talent and gifted potential in diverse populations: committed professionals, nontraditional identification methods for finding students, research-based interventions to nurture and support students' talents, and other essential elements that show promise for finding and supporting students who have historically been absent in gifted programs. An overview of these four major components is provided here, and they are addressed further throughout this text.

Committed Professionals. Young Scholars requires a school-wide commitment on the part of all educators to find and develop talent in students from populations that have historically been overlooked. The principals of Young Scholars schools are committed to increasing the number of learners from traditionally underserved populations who receive advanced academic services at their schools, and principals play a key role in the success of the model. They view themselves as instructional leaders and champions for the model and for their students. These leaders serve as strong advocates for the students, provide ongoing support to the teachers, and ensure that year after year the young scholars are clustered with teachers who know how to nurture and develop their gifted potential. Across a district implementing the Young Scholars Model, principals meet several times a year to collaborate, share ideas, and tackle the challenges and concerns that must be addressed as they implement the model at their schools.

An important designation in each school is a Young Scholars advocate. This could be a gifted and talented resource teacher, instructional coach, or other teacher leader who has a passion for finding and serving young scholars and a willingness to participate in and lead the professional learning efforts that are needed for successful implementation of the model. This individual can also play a leading role in developing and sustaining a Young Scholars leadership team that facilitates the ongoing planning, implementation, and evaluation of the model in the school. Often, the person who takes on this role is a lead or resource teacher who works directly with students some of the time and directly with other teachers as well, supporting the integration of aspects of the model consistently across the school.

Teachers plan and share lessons, curricula, resources, and strategies that support their efforts to find and nurture gifted potential. They also meet as grade-level teams to design and implement differentiated lessons that challenge young scholars to think on a higher level and study advanced content through projects, research, and extensions of the general education curriculum. The teachers and specialists understand that the success of the model is dependent on their collaborative efforts.

All professionals within a school are part of the commitment to find and nurture young scholars. This includes not only school leaders and classroom teachers, but also school counselors, resource teachers, and others who have opportunities to observe and recognize talent potential. The commitment of the educators throughout the school is supported by efforts from the leadership team to develop a shared culture around supporting access and talent development for learners.

Find and Identify. Young scholars are students who are not likely to be considered for gifted programs using traditional methods of identification, and who, without that opportunity, are less likely to pursue advanced levels of learning on their own. Historically, these students have lacked access to gifted services, advocates for their high potential, and affirmation of their advanced abilities. The model begins as a talent development program in grades K–2; however, young scholars may be identified at any grade level. Young scholars are identified by principals, classroom teachers, education specialists, and/or gifted and talented resource teachers through an examination of student portfolios and performance-based assessments. School professionals work together to find and nurture advanced potential in young learners, employing high-quality curriculum written for advanced learners as an important part of the effort to seek talent.

Teachers at Young Scholars schools participate in extensive professional learning activities that focus on the importance of considering the diversity of background experiences that young scholars bring to school. This enables teachers to recognize gifted behaviors in the context of prior opportunities. Teachers learn instructional strategies designed to elicit high-level responses and ways to record evidence of advanced potential through observations, anecdotal records, and paper or digital portfolios of student work that capture evidence of growth over time.

Students are given multiple opportunities to demonstrate academic strengths, and teachers at the schools continuously review and consider multiple forms of data as they search for and build on student strengths to find and nurture emerging talent in young scholars. As one teacher stated, "I have discovered that there are many methods one can utilize to identify giftedness other than merely relying on standardized test results. I am now a strong supporter of portfolio presentations and anecdotal records to illustrate a child's abilities and talents."

Nurture, Guide, and Support. The Young Scholars Model promotes the notion of continuous intellectual growth beginning in kindergarten. Although all children need learning experiences that prepare them to succeed in a complex and competitive world, students from underrepresented backgrounds may be less likely to engage in the experiences that are relevant to advanced academic success as compared to some of their peers, and the school can help to fill in the experience gaps. Therefore, young scholars participate in specific interventions designed to develop and nurture their advanced potential. The teachers in Young Scholars schools learn how to infuse more rigor in lessons that connect to the students' diverse cultural, economic, and linguistic backgrounds while they help the students gain proficiency in reading and mathematics.

The learning experiences that teachers provide for young scholars promote a climate in which advanced knowledge, understandings, and skills are developed, guided, and supported. Teachers work together to design lessons that connect new knowledge and understandings to students' personal background and life experiences. Poems, stories, and plays that contain dialect, relevant role models, and varying cultural lifestyles are integrated throughout the curriculum. Authors, artists, inventors, scientists, mathematicians, and other leaders from diverse backgrounds who have made significant contributions to society are infused into the entire learning experience. The teachers find that when students are given the opportunity to study the diverse group of leaders who have changed the world for the better, they realize that the traits and characteristics these people possess cross all lines of color, class, and culture, and their personal aspirations are enhanced.

Young scholars gain important skills and confidence as they create questions, search for answers, and share what they learn through products and presentations that they design. As their confidence increases, their motivation and willingness to take risks increase as well. For example, a group of first-grade young scholars created a PowerPoint presentation to teach kindergarten students all that they had learned about insects. As they designed and created their presentation, the first-grade students became experts on their topic and were excited to share their knowledge with their younger peers. Another group of young scholars in fifth and sixth grade explored the concept of a watershed as they learned their watershed address and discovered their connection to a nearby bay through their local streams. After an in-depth study of the watershed and problems that ensue when it is not protected, the students decided to take action and share with other students ways that they could help improve the health of the watershed and save a local bay. The young scholars worked together and designed a school television show on the importance of protecting the local watershed. This experience allowed them to make a real-world connection and to see themselves as problem solvers of an issue that impacted their lives and their community.

 Essential Elements. Learning experiences for the students in Young Scholars schools are coupled with professional learning opportunities for educators and outreach to parents.

Professional learning for teachers at Young Scholars schools includes culturally responsive teaching, how to identify talent potential in diverse populations, gifted education pedagogy, and how to observe and record evidence in student portfolios. Teachers participate in school teams focused on the goals of the Young Scholars Model, and they engage in collaborative learning and planning to respond to students' needs.

Families are invited to be partners in their child's education. Before-school, afterschool, and evening events are arranged to give parents multiple opportunities to learn about the Young Scholars Model, what it means for their child's school experiences, and how they can best support their child. Many schools provide books and information in multiple languages. Some school systems create a parent resource center to house these materials for parents. They also offer parent academies on various topics. Families are invited to help with classroom projects, attend student presentations, and accompany the children on field trips. Through active involvement they gain a better understanding of the advanced learning opportunities that are available to their children and how they can provide advocacy and support.

A summer school program for young scholars provides the students with important learning opportunities that are extended and enriched. The summer school teachers are prepared to implement a highly challenging curriculum that includes concept-based instruction, enrichment opportunities, field trips, and guest speakers. Summer school classes are multiage, and basic skills are strengthened through learning opportunities that challenge the students to think and apply knowledge on a higher, more complex level.

In the fall, each school site makes a concerted effort to provide young scholars with opportunities to grow and develop with intellectual peers from similar backgrounds. Many schools cluster the young scholars with teachers who are endorsed in gifted education and/or those who have engaged in extensive professional learning and practice around the model. Young Scholars schools also create additional afterschool or in-school opportunities for the young scholars in order to continue to nurture their potential.

Schools that implement the Young Scholars Model experience changes in school culture and their perception of who should participate in advanced classes. The four components come together in an integrated way to help these schools move beyond a reliance on test scores to a multidimensional view of advanced potential that includes a profile of academic strengths and talents. The changes in school culture and the multilayered structures that support this change from within create a climate of learning in which every child is continuously assessed and nurtured toward reaching their full potential.

The model takes time to develop in a particular school or district. Throughout this text, we provide guidelines for initiating and sustaining aspects of the model. We offer some questions that school teams can ask themselves about their specific context and how to tailor the model locally, and we provide indicators for progress in implementation of the model. These indicators include rubrics for the four major components of the model at the elementary and secondary level (see Chapter 2 and Chapter 8), as well as additional checklists and guidelines. In most chapters, we have included a chart demonstrating indicators of levels of implementation, to be considered as "entry points" and "growth edges" showing stages of progress over time.

Voices From the Field

I have been a very passionate supporter of the Young Scholars program since its beginning. Being given the opportunity to work with students who were identified as young scholars inspired me to pursue my advanced academics endorsement. Furthering my knowledge of meeting their academic needs was very important.

I love to see students think and learn. As a Young Scholars teacher, I strive to provide instruction that allows students to question, investigate, and engage in learning activities, comfortably. This allows students to think outside the box, be risk-takers without being judged or ridiculed, and connect with their peers on a higher level. Through their conversations, ideas, self-directed projects, etc., students are always connecting what they are learning to their own experiences. I have had students write poems, songs, and plays; design a costume or backdrop for a play or reader's theater; create a new holiday, celebration, community and/or town; write a "Tiny Tale" and create the characters; write stories from a different perspective; and express their ideas through art and dance.

I am often visited by many former students. I love hearing about their accomplishments, goals, and dreams.

Two students come to mind who were in my first- and second-grade classes. Both young ladies graduated from high school with honors in 2014. I was invited to their graduation, but due to my teaching responsibilities, I was unable to attend. I did receive pictures and phone calls of excitement! Both students received scholarships to Virginia universities.

One student graduated from Marymount University with honors. She received a BS degree in nursing and is currently working at Children's National Hospital as a pediatric nurse on the surgical trauma /COVID-19 unit. She will be transitioning to the COVID-19 emergency response team for her county health department soon.

The second student graduated from Virginia Tech with honors. She received a BS in sustainable biomaterials and minored in green engineering. She is working at ICF International as a public policy analyst and plans to pursue a master's degree in environmental science.

Both young ladies were young scholars. They were identified at an early age. They were nurtured, valued, respected, and encouraged to do their best, be their best, and persevere as young scholars.

We have remained in touch since they were in my class. They would always visit me before, during, and after each school year from elementary through college. Now, we try to meet twice a year to catch up, reminisce, and laugh. I am always touched when one of them will thank me, followed by "Because of you, Ms. B., we made it; we are where we are because of you."

I believe the Young Scholars Model is one of the best approaches for identifying, supporting, and challenging those students who have high academic potential, but may not be considered for an advanced academic program. Teaching these students has allowed me to be their advocate. To provide learning experiences that will strengthen a child's mind and help them apply this knowledge on a higher level is astounding. This helps open doors to their life, their education, and a world of opportunities.

—Vici Bolton, primary elementary teacher at a Young Scholars school

Transitioning From Labels to Services

Over time, educational reforms and a focus on best practices have highlighted the fact that many educational practices that were once reserved for gifted students would benefit all learners. In addition, a focus on matching services to individual strengths and needs illustrates the overall need for advanced academic services that are not a one-size-fits-all program. Best practice in gifted education requires a range of services to develop exceptional potential in a diverse group of advanced learners within the school and district environment. Through teacher collaboration and varied instructional groupings, classroom teachers are able to extend and enrich curriculum and instruction for students who are ready for additional challenge or acceleration in one or more subjects.

The Young Scholars Model supports the notion of providing equity of opportunity to all students so that any child who has an exceptional ability to think, reason, and problem solve will be able to receive gifted services. Because the context in which students learn and the expectations of their teachers are critical determiners of whether or not advanced academic potential is nurtured and developed, young scholars are provided with powerful learning experiences that challenge and motivate them to move beyond existing molds and reach new heights.

The model encapsulates key components that are interdependent and integral to finding and nurturing gifted potential in diverse populations. These components include advocates for students who have been historically underrepresented, access to research-based interventions and high-level curriculum, and affirmation and development of gifted potential. Implementation of the model leads to systemic change and a school environment that encourages continuous learning and advanced intellectual growth. Early identification coupled with early intervention allows each Young Scholars school to provide learning experiences that increase the students' self-efficacy. The teachers, specialists, and administrators are student advocates, and they provide ongoing support to the young scholars as they prepare them for the challenging curriculum and instruction that advanced academic programs offer throughout their school years.

Situating Young Scholars Within Overall Talent Development, Identification, and Differentiated Services

One key misconception that sometimes arises around Young Scholars is that it functions as a program separately from a district's gifted program. In truth, it is a thread through district gifted programming that provides wraparound support for students from underrepresented populations from the stages of access to opportunities that reveal talent, to identification, to ensuring success while the young scholar receives gifted services. The talent development focus is a critical way of thinking that includes frequent opportunities to not only spot, but also develop talent.

Figure 2 represents the critical nature of a strong talent development model that focuses on student identity, access to rigor, and student agency for all students and situates Young Scholars as a system of support for some students that feeds culturally responsive identification and differentiated services. Together, a strong talent development agenda that includes attention to historically underrepresented populations will eliminate the ways educators are currently leaving potential talent unactualized for some students.

Figure 2

Young Scholars as a Component of District Talent Development and Its Relationship to Gifted Identification and Services

Talent Development		Culturally Responsive Identification Practices	Differentiation for Advanced Learner Needs

Talent Development
For all K–12 classrooms and students

Student Identity	Access to Rigor	Student Agency
• Identify and nurture strengths and interests • Explore career connections and identity	• Provide all students with access to deeper learning curriculum and strategies • Scaffold for success	• Apply culturally responsive teaching principles • Cultivate attitudes and mindsets that empower

Systems of Support for Some Students: Young Scholars

• Implement all parts of the Young Scholars Model with fidelity:
  Committed Professionals - Find/Identify
  Nurture/Guide/Support - Essential Elements

• Psychosocial interventions for students and educator professional learning to close access gaps in advanced academics for underrepresented subgroups (e.g., twice-exceptional, ELLs, low-income backgrounds, and Black or Hispanic)

Culturally Responsive Identification Practices

• Equity-focused screening policies and tools, including holistic and contextual consideration of data from multiple sources

• Multiple entry points and monitoring

Young Scholars

• Young scholars are identified for advanced academic services at the elementary level and are enrolled in advanced coursework in secondary school

Differentiation for Advanced Learner Needs

• Differentiated content, process, product (e.g., time and intensity of depth and complexity, ascending levels of intellectual demand, integration of social-emotional curriculum)

• Grouping and placement considerations (e.g., pair with a trained teacher and a cluster of peers with similar academic needs)

Young Scholars

• Provide supplementary enrichment and support for success

• Opportunities for cluster grouping of young scholars with teachers who have deeper training in the model

How does a strong talent development program increase equity in K–12 gifted programs?

How does a strong talent development focus benefit all students? How does it improve identification for gifted services? How does it increase the likelihood of maximizing student potential into actualized talent through differentiated services?

Young Scholars began with a small pilot of 30 students from one Title I school in 2001. Today there are more than 15,000 identified young scholars in grades K–12 in the original district who receive advocacy, access, and affirmation of their talent potential from the school district (Horn, 2018). Many young scholars visit or write letters to tell former teachers about the impact of the model on their learning and their lives. One student recently wrote to a former teacher:

> I hope you know how much Young Scholars shaped my life. . . .
> I am now at [the University of Virginia] and am going into com-
> puter science engineering. . . . My love for science and math
> comes from my Young Scholars roots. . . . Young Scholars was
> such a great part of my life and I am so grateful for the time
> and compassion you gave and showed me through my elemen-
> tary school years. And I can honestly say that I will be a young
> scholar for life.

Chapter 2

School and District Leadership

> Vision without action is merely a dream. Action without vision just passes the time. Vision with action can change the world.
>
> —Joel Barker

Successful implementation of the Young Scholars Model depends on a commitment from multiple stakeholders and a strong investment from district and school leadership. Leaders at the school and district level shape the model's effectiveness when they invite and sustain collaboration among professional teams. Such collaboration not only promotes the goals of the model, but also ensures its long-term growth and success. Further, leaders who are successful with the model are able to communicate and encourage a big-picture vision that demonstrates how the Young Scholars Model aligns and intersects with broader school and district goals to promote equity, excellence, academic achievement, and success.

We believe . . .

- ❧ Alignment between district and school leadership is key to closing excellence gaps.
- ❧ Shared leadership within a school benefits students, engages staff, and encourages an innovative school and community environment.
- ❧ Ongoing professional learning and networking opportunities for school leaders are critical to continuous improvement.
- ❧ Effective leaders engage in ongoing evaluation to ensure continuous improvement in schools and across the district.
- ❧ Leadership emerges not only from individuals in leadership positions, but also from other members of school teams working collaboratively toward shared goals.

In this chapter . . .

- ❧ We explore the important role that leadership plays throughout model implementation.
- ❧ We explain the value of distributive leadership within a school and across a district.
- ❧ We share strategies that lead to a school and district culture that supports and nurtures talent development in all populations of learners.
- ❧ We share ideas for introducing the Young Scholars Model to a school or district.

School and district leadership are linked to all four parts of the Young Scholars Model:

Committed Professionals. School and district leaders create and work toward a shared vision to address the problem of underrepresentation of specific groups of students in gifted programming and to ensure schools are not letting talent slip through the cracks.

Find and Identify. School and district leaders communicate the shared vision through words and actions that embody the belief that each staff member has a role in scouting for talent and potential. School and district leaders maintain a consistent message that focuses on seeking talent in learners from all backgrounds and supporting talent development through a focus on nurturing academic strengths.

 **Nurture, Guide, and Support.** School and district leaders examine whether there are unintended or systemic barriers to opportunities that would reveal or cultivate talent. They provide support to remove such barriers and promote increased access. School leaders convey that each staff member must not only have high expectations of the students, but also provide challenging learning experiences so that the students will have high expectations for themselves. Leaders consider the needs of young scholars in grouping practices, decisions around curriculum and instruction, and providing purposeful wraparound services to ensure student success.

 Essential Elements. School and district leaders set a vision and goals for strong implementation of the Young Scholars Model, use data to inform areas for continuous improvement, and offer professional learning that deepens understanding of the systemic issues underlying the problem of underrepresentation. Leaders expect all educators to play a role in developing talent and closing excellence gaps. Leaders offer before- and afterschool enrichment experiences and/or summer school programs designed to develop talent in underrepresented populations. They also cultivate an inclusive and welcoming school climate that engages families as partners in the development of their child's potential.

Why a Leadership Focus?

The Young Scholars Model rests on a schoolwide commitment to equity, access, and talent development. Such a commitment requires substantial work on the part of school leaders to invite and communicate vision, promote shared understandings, and support practices that will facilitate progress toward goals. It also requires a network within and beyond the school that sustains a collective culture focused on equity. School and district leaders have the opportunity and authority to initiate and sustain a Young Scholars approach. Further, the leadership emerging from individuals across school teams promotes continuous improvement and growth-focused implementation in all aspects of the model.

The Young Scholars Model is most powerful when structures exist to ensure support for students from kindergarten through high school graduation. It is important not only to consider the development of the student over time and instill high expectations, but also to develop confidence and navigational and problem-solving tools that are needed for success during and beyond high school. In pursuit of closing achievement and excellence gaps, school systems need to examine existing opportunity gaps and ensure that all students have access to the learning opportunities that will develop their potential into actualized talent. A district with an equity focus will consider evidence of student talents in a context that recognizes the unequal landscape that affects students even before kindergarten. A focus on potential, access, and growth that is not limited by grade-level standards will promote talent across all student groups.

Efforts to examine and reform structures, sustain and communicate a consistent focus on equity, and encourage a mindset focused on access and growth all rest on the involvement and commitment of school and district leaders, including those in formal leadership positions and those who demonstrate leadership from any role. At the district level, it is important that the superintendent and central office leaders incorporate the Young Scholars Model into their overall plans and goals for addressing the issue of equity. School board members should be briefed on the implementation of the model and the ways their decisions support its success.

For example, in one district, school board members were invited to hear a panel of gifted resource teachers and classroom teachers discuss the ways that coaching from the resource teacher broadened the classroom teacher's pedagogical toolbox to include increases to deeper learning curriculum experiences. This compelled the board to increase funding so that all Title I schools would have a full-time resource teacher. In another district, board members were invited to visit Young Scholars summer school classes, where they saw firsthand the value of this summer opportunity. The projects and presentations that the students were engaged in prompted a board member to work with a local foundation to secure more funding to increase the number of schools able to offer summer enrichment opportunities that were free to young scholars.

The Role of Distributed Leadership: District, School, Teachers, and Context

All roles in the school and system, including those that represent formal leadership positions and those that do not, have leadership potential. Individuals in any role may influence efforts to create an equity-driven culture committed to finding and nurturing students from historically underrepresented populations.

Teachers, principals, and district leaders—individuals in all of these positions contribute to a sustainable Young Scholars Model by employing their spheres of influence and strategically identifying areas that will create and strengthen an environment committed to talent development in all students. The Young Scholars Model requires leading for learning, which is most powerful when leadership is distributed among all levels of an organization.

An effective and sustainable model requires alignment, coherence, and focus, with measured progress, toward a shared vision. The central office ensures alignment of curriculum and assessment resources, funding and opportunities for professional learning for teachers, and support for school-based instructional leaders focused on equity leadership. School-based administrators engage with the central office for instructional and equity leadership support; align school goals, structures, and actions; and include measures of progress in school improvement plans. Teachers participate in professional learning about components of the model, enacting a collaborative network beyond individual classrooms that promotes collegial accountability, and provide feedback to school leaders about ideas for schoolwide improvement or areas of needed support.

Instructional and equity leadership positions are inherently distributed to different staff and throughout different levels of the organization so that leadership is located in the relationships among people in a variety of positions more than in specific individuals (Knapp et al., 2014). This distributed leadership approach not only brings together a conceptual notion of shared leadership, but also backs it with organizational structures that coordinate and make alignment more likely. Although more stakeholders are involved in continuously improving the system aligned with vision, forms of leadership depend on active engagement of those in formal authority to organize and coordinate aligned efforts (Leithwood, 2012).

Fundamentally, a district's or school's decision to adopt the Young Scholars Model is driven by a leadership perspective that values equity, access, and talent development. This decision follows a leader's recognition of a gap in identification and/or performance and a realization of what is sacrificed and lost without intentional improvement—loss of potential, missed opportunities to explore interest areas and consider career pathways, and failure to activate the promise of education as the great equalizer. Some schools may feel the representation issue is too complex and consider eliminating gifted programming as a solution. Others will realize that elimination of opportunities offered within gifted programs will reduce visibility of the problem but will not eliminate the problem; rather, such an approach has the potential to further hold back students whose families may be less likely to be able to access enrichment opportunities outside of school. Although it requires more effort, a focus on proactive approaches around recognizing and nurturing talent will provide more answers to the questions of how educators ensure equity while also pursuing excellence.

A successful implementation of the Young Scholars Model requires commitment to the ethics of finding and nurturing potential in diverse student populations and a shared approach to leadership. Strong leaders need to know the "why" behind programs in their district or school and regularly assess alignment of actions to goals. Further, the model relies on collaborative efforts of professionals and families to support student access and growth, and thus it rests on leadership that is shared and distributed. New demands for collaboration and teamwork necessitate a shift in the traditional power structure. The emphasis on top-down power is replaced with an emphasis on shared power and the use of power to empower others. Leadership behaviors are incorporated at all levels of the school system, from superintendent to directors to principals to teachers. When leadership is shared, teachers and administrators work together to build and achieve a dynamic vision that is flexible and responsive to the needs of the community.

The initial spark for the decision to adopt the Young Scholars Model is often driven from a values standpoint and requires a moral leadership perspective that centers decision making and resources around equity. This spark may come from a principal who feels the demographics of those identified for gifted services in their school do not reflect their belief that exceptional potential and talent exist in all subgroups of students, including those who are learning English or those who are currently from low-income backgrounds. It may come from a teacher who has noted that an ability test score does not capture the advanced reasoning skills that they see in a student. Wherever it emerges, the decision to employ the Young Scholars Model is one that grows from a personal commitment to progress beyond an insufficient paradigm that has clear gaps in identification methods, due possibly to overreliance on test scores or advantages from prior opportunities to learn that mask talent in some students before they enter and while they are in the K–12 system. This decision to implement the model must then be accompanied by a commitment to building the culture and shared leadership support to promote its successful implementation.

Strengthening School Culture for Talent Development

To support implementing the Young Scholars Model and creating a culture in which all teachers feel invested in closing excellence gaps, leaders need to consider strategies for capacity and culture building as well as accountability connected to the purposes of the model. It is important to be explicit about how the model connects to larger district goals, other initiatives, and school improvement plans. It is equally important to provide time for school staff to explore and discuss these connections to support their commitment to finding and nurturing potential in historically underrepresented student groups.

The Young Scholars Model relies on a network of committed professionals in the school. Naturally, there may be some leaders within the school, such as the school-based administrator or a gifted resource teacher, who may lead with starting the model or having teams examine areas for growth, but over time leadership for the model will grow into a school culture such that thinking about the needs of young scholars is an organic and authentic part of school and team planning. The initial steps of exploring how the model will work in a particular school should include engaging several staff members representing different roles as a leadership team for planning implementation. These individuals can serve as champions for the process and work to bring along and support colleagues as the model moves forward.

A leadership team can work to nurture an environment for distributed leadership, with simultaneous attention to creating and sustaining professional learning communities and the adult development theory considerations that undergird their potential strength to shift school culture. In *Leading Change Together: Developing Educator Capacity Within Schools and Systems*, authors Drago-Severson and Blum-DeStefano (2018) discussed the importance of several key considerations in developing supportive environments for capacity and leadership:

- understand adult development and its role in systemic change and continuous school improvement (i.e., meet adults where they are because it is important to recognize and respond to a starting place to bring people along with change),
- make concrete connections between theory and practice with real-life examples that people can relate to,
- challenge and recognize "growth edges" in making meaning amid diverse perspectives and complex issues because some of the ideas may challenge existing paradigms and practices,
- differentiate elements of adult learning because different members of a school staff have different needs in response to their varied roles and levels of readiness, and
- build trust and inspire leadership through collaboration and capacity building while recognizing each person's unique talents and experiences.

The professional learning that needs to take place to create a strong Young Scholars Model within a school includes components that are both informational—what we know—and transformational—how we know. Topics around equity and underrepresentation in gifted programming call on adult learners to examine transformational topics alongside the informational. Informational topics might concern which resources to use or what behaviors to look for, while transformational topics will concern what the members of the school community believe about student potential and the role of schools in developing talent. Transformational learning requires a safe environment for adults to discuss the complexities of these topics with collaborative support and trust (Drago-Severson & Blum-DeStefano, 2018).

Promoting a school culture supportive of the Young Scholars Model's focus on equity and talent development rests on building buy-in, and such buy-in may emerge in part from closer examination of the available data. The leadership team facilitates a process of looking at who is participating in gifted services and other advanced academic opportunities in the school or district. Ideally, this process should be one that is open and invitational, giving teachers a chance to look at the evidence and come to key conclusions about the current context. When school staff members are not given time to build their understanding and recognize underrepresentation issues for themselves, there may be lower buy-in to the model and its potential to support talent development and access for students.

A second critical part of building a supportive school culture is consistent and clear attention to how Young Scholars aligns with other initiatives and is not just another added effort. Schools often suffer from "initiative fatigue" if too many different efforts are occurring at once, giving the staff too many responsibilities and new resources to juggle. Thus, it is important to show how implementation of the Young Scholars Model enhances and aligns with other priorities and goals within the school, instead of being separate from them.

Getting Started: Guiding Questions for Leaders

Depending on the roles of the educators who initiate consideration of the Young Scholars Model, there are a number of key questions and data sources to review as a foundation for getting started. Further, leaders in different positions may set goals that focus on different aspects of the model to support equity of access and talent development. In this section, we provide some sample questions and considerations for leaders in different roles as they think about how to implement the Young Scholars Model in their areas of influence.

District Leadership

One key consideration for district leaders is examining existing goals and systems for advanced academic services and determining the degree to which increasing access and promoting talent development are clear parts of those goals and systems. A stated goal related to talent development provides an important foundation for the Young Scholars Model.

District-level leaders should also focus on how networks at the district level can support the goals of the model and promote innovation and improvement in talent development efforts. For example, it is important for district leaders who are responsible for gifted and advanced academic services to connect and collaborate with the leaders who supervise instruction in specific content areas as well as the leaders who facilitate key equity initiatives. Such relationships promote the alignment of efforts to address the needs of learners and the educators who work with them.

Some guiding questions that district-level leaders may use to facilitate reflection and conversation around the Young Scholars Model include the following:

- How do you use data to examine gaps in access and opportunity in your district? What data sources are regularly examined, and to what degree do these efforts focus on advanced-level learning and learners?
- How can you effectively and concretely demonstrate the alignment of Young Scholars with other district goals, priorities, and initiatives?
- In what ways do district policies around identification for advanced academic services incorporate alternative identification methods that enable a focus on the strengths of students who are historically underrepresented in gifted/advanced academic services?
- What is your assessment of the current mindsets of school leaders around the ideas of talent development and equity? How might you learn more about their beliefs and values on these issues?
- What structures does your district have that will support starting or strengthening the Young Scholars Model? What are the gaps and challenges that might present barriers? What additional structures might be needed?
- What schools or teams might be early adopters with whom you could work more closely?
- What existing professional learning structures and initiatives might be useful for supporting educators in understanding and implementing the model?

      ❦ What communication systems will support highlighting best practices and increasing the visibility of successful efforts?

      ❦ What systems and supports will help schools in staying abreast of the research and literature around promoting equity and talent development?

      ❦ What access do you have to a broader network for support and collaboration?

School-Level Leadership

School administrators seeking to initiate or support the Young Scholars Model in their building also benefit from a thorough consideration of key questions around existing systems, current data, and school culture. It is useful for school administrators to consider their networks and relationships with other principals and district leaders, and how those relationships can guide and facilitate effective implementation of the model. Within a school, it is important to consider both the explicit and implicit messages that the staff receives and whether they align with the school leader's vision for pursuing the goals of the Young Scholars Model. Some guiding questions for school administrators include the following:

      ❦ How do you use data to examine gaps in access and opportunity in your school? How do you involve others in examining these data?

      ❦ What leadership practices do you employ to support a school culture in which a critical mass of school staff are committed to closing excellence gaps?

      ❦ How can you effectively and concretely communicate the alignment of the Young Scholars goals with other initiatives and efforts within the school?

      ❦ How do you prioritize discussions around the importance of access to deeper learning strategies or the observation of exceptional behaviors among school staff? What space and time do you allocate to these discussions?

      ❦ What do you highlight in terms of achievements and success stories within the school?

      ❦ What focus areas does the school have around professional learning, and how is key content related to the Young Scholars Model presented?

      ❦ What systems are in place to promote family engagement, and who are the families that participate?

      ❦ Beyond your school walls, how do you share your vision and improvement journey with your colleagues?

Voices From the Field

The school-based administrator has a critical role to play in creating and maintaining the structures that allow for early identification and ongoing nurturing of gifted behaviors in students via the Young Scholars Model. Principals are constantly navigating a wide variety of responsibilities and really need to be able to plan key school improvement initiatives with stakeholders, communicate expectations with clarity, and monitor the progress and implementation with fidelity. In our county, we are fortunate to have assigned Advanced Academic Resource Teachers (AARTs) to lead the learning in our schools, while central office support staff provide ongoing professional learning opportunities for school administrators and teachers. School leaders benefit from opportunities to engage in learning around research-based practices that help us understand where we need to go next in terms of our "Access to Rigor" planning efforts. Many of these learning opportunities take place in conjunction with our AARTs, and the best opportunities include time for processing and strategic planning.

Initial goal-setting meetings and recurring progress meetings between the administrator and the AART are important opportunities to develop a shared understanding of what is needed and to allow for access to opportunities for advanced learning among all populations of students. Successful AARTs work with the building principal to plan for the best way to identify gifted potential in our young scholars. Scheduling is a critical component and must include plenty of time to plan with teachers and to support the delivery of instruction by modeling, coteaching, and observing with follow-up coaching conversations and feedback. AARTs need to find the appropriate entry points with teachers who may have different readiness levels or even for those who are resistant due to skill deficits or differing viewpoints on what students might be able to handle. The development of a culture of learning and collaboration to make this happen is the responsibility of every staff member, but always starts with a clearly communicated vision and ongoing visibility of the building principal to encourage and explain the work. Even the best instructional leaders [AARTs] would struggle in a culture that lacks interdependence.

When AARTs can spend the time needed to model lessons in the classroom, they are able to notice and name gifted behaviors in the moment and have follow-up conversations with classroom teachers. This supports the early identification of gifted patterns in students and helps classroom teachers learn about what these behaviors look and sound like, while helping them to elicit these behaviors through their lesson planning. When teachers see how they can embed critical and creative thinking and other strategies into their planning in a way that supports deeper meaning and content acquisition, they are more willing to stretch themselves and to devote the time needed. As teachers become more and more confident in utilizing their new tools for engagement, their ability to recognize gifted behaviors increases along with their ability to advocate for advanced learning opportunities for their students. Principals need to support this work in particular by visiting classrooms, noticing and sharing these connections to deep understanding of content, acknowledging the appropriate and professional risk taken, and highlighting and sharing the accomplishments [and failures] along the way. When these highlights are realized, teachers ask for more and more time to work on utilization of advanced curriculum, and principals need to be ready to make it a priority in common planning and "Collaborative Learning Team" structures.

The exposure to advanced curriculum, in the primary grades especially, will certainly go a long way in supporting the identification of our young scholars, although nurturing their potential is equally as important for a successful program. Over the years, we have found that the appropriate balance of time includes more opportunities for direct instruction to our young scholars during the primary years upon initial identification. Our AART pulls groups weekly in grades K–2 and every other week in the upper grades, while maintaining a variety of cocurricular experiences in the way of field trips and afterschool programming. With identified young scholars participating in all levels of the [gifted services] continuum, the ongoing success of our Young Scholars program has been largely dependent on our ability to build capacity in our entire staff to use advanced curriculum with all of our students. Our AART uses a crosswalk tool to demonstrate connections between content and the most appropriate advanced academic resources that complement it. She will provide the autonomy for teams to select the focus for collaboration and then make the time to plan with teachers and/ or teams. Collaborative planning focused on the identification of access points, differentiation strategies, and appropriate scaffolds is necessary to achieve any real momentum, although this concentrated planning and support needs to be coupled with support for effective delivery of instruction as well. AARTs need to be empowered to see this learning cycle through in order to really assess the impact of the teaching and learning using this strategy for job-embedded professional learning.

—Paul Basdekis, principal of a Young Scholars school

Teacher Leadership

Teacher leaders play an important role in sparking and sustaining a school-wide commitment to the Young Scholars Model. Teachers may have the best opportunities to observe and record evidence of student strengths and to recognize where talent might be being overlooked, and their close relationships with students support building trust in pursuing advanced academic opportunities. Further, networks of teachers can work together to try out approaches to drawing out and responding to talents in students from underserved groups. Some of the questions teachers might consider and bring to a broader leadership team include the following:

- What observations have you made about strengths and needs in students from traditionally underserved populations?
- What ideas do you have for expanding access to instructional approaches that have been used in gifted education to find students who have not yet been identified?
- How might you document your observations of student strengths in ways that may not have been part of existing identification protocols?
- How do you show student growth over time to capture aptitude and achievement beyond assessments?
- What scaffolds and supports do you anticipate students might need to be successful in advanced learning opportunities or in understanding pathways to their academic and career goals?

Voices From the Field

Young Scholars is a schoolwide effort.

I recall approaching my first year as an Advanced Academic Resource Teacher (AART) with a lot of ideas, particularly when it came to how I wanted to implement Young Scholars at my school. I remember sharing some ideas with someone, and this person encouraged me to not do it all alone. This was good advice. I asked around to some teachers to see if they would consider being a part of the Young Scholars Committee and then emailed the staff to see if anyone would be interested in taking a close look at our school's data through the lens of programmatic equity. Our first meeting had 12 people in attendance, including our principal and assistant principal. We started our meeting by taking a look at national trends in gifted education and then challenged one another by reflecting upon our own implicit biases when considering our own advanced academic recommendations. Our next meeting focused on taking a look at the Young Scholars Implementation Rubric and collectively deciding our course of action as a school.

We still have a lot of work to do as a Young Scholars school, but I love that my librarian, STEAM teacher, or reading recovery teacher will send me an email to check in about a student, who might stand out in their specific domain, but whose talent perhaps might have been overlooked using traditional measures of assessment. I love that I can sit back during middle school recommendation meetings because my counselor has worked alongside our young scholars after school the entire year and can specifically address each child's strengths and advocate for a child's rigorous class placement without my having to open my mouth. I appreciate that I have a kindergarten teacher who will text me and say, "You've got to stop by and see what this child just did. She is definitely a young scholar—look at her critical and creative thinking." I love how even parent volunteers have stepped in to help run our Young Scholars afterschool program, and when the pandemic hit, they were ready and willing to hand deliver care packages to all of our scholars. Over the summer, eight teachers took our county course on Young Scholars to further their understanding of the model. Our staff and community are committed to identifying and nurturing the talent of our young scholars, which is a relief because the work cannot be done alone.

—Jackie Kwon, Advanced Academic Resource Teacher

Launching the Process: Building a Team and a Plan

As leaders reflect on questions such as those outlined previously and examine data as a foundation for a Young Scholars initiative, a key next step is to bring together a team of individuals within the school who will serve as the organizers and champions as the plan and implementation of the model move ahead. Such a team should include administrators, teachers, and other personnel who can support the overall effort to prioritize talent development and equity of access to advanced experiences.

Some discussion questions for initial meetings of the Young Scholars team might include the following:

- What are our school's strengths related to promoting equity and encouraging talent development? What aspects of our school culture are supportive of a strength-based focus and a growth mindset? What are some of our needs in these areas?

∾ What evidence supports the need and opportunity for implementing Young Scholars in the school?

∾ What are the existing initiatives in the school and district related to equity? How can we demonstrate alignment with the goals and strategies of those initiatives?

∾ What are the existing goals and structures for professional learning, and where are there opportunities to align the Young Scholars Model with them?

∾ What approaches do we currently use for grouping students in classrooms, and how might we make use of cluster grouping to support the Young Scholars Model?

∾ What are some possible incentives for staff to be leaders in getting the Young Scholars Model started?

∾ What patterns of family engagement do we typically see in our school, and what are our needs in that area?

∾ What are some potential areas in which we might experience pushback, and how can we respond productively?

As the team considers questions like these and discusses plans for launching a Young Scholars program, several important activities may be part of their work:

∾ gathering tips and feedback from other Young Scholars schools;

∾ documenting recent and current data;

∾ drafting goals, steps, and timelines for getting started with each key aspect of the model (i.e., professional learning, family engagement, curricular decision making);

∾ considering what benchmarks will be used to evaluate progress; and

∾ encouraging potential "champions" to join the planning team.

These efforts can be supported by existing resources that provide an effective way for the team to self-assess and connect outcomes to specific growth strategies. Although the model is purposefully designed for flexibility, many schools experience increased clarity of specific actions over time through organizers or rubrics. The originators of the model observed over time and multiple school settings that it would help school teams to have some concrete examples of what implementation looked like on a journey from beginning stages to a fully realized model with a strong commitment from all stakeholders. Further, such examples and organizing documents can support school teams in the wake of changing leadership or teacher turnover.

Figure 3 is a sample Young Scholars Model implementation rubric[1]. This rubric allows schools to plan and self-assess their progress from launching to developing to highly functioning in the four major components of the model: committed professionals; find and identify; nurture, guide, and support; and essential elements. Articulating a starting point (launching) and an ideal state (highly functioning) helped schools determine where they were and where they needed to go to fully realize the power of the model. From the beginning of the planning process and throughout implementation, teams may keep a focus on intended goals and outcomes by reviewing the rubric.

One way that the rubric might be used is to have several members of the team self-assess where they believe the school is in the four areas of the model, coupled with a discussion with school-based administrators about their assessment. From that discussion, the team could determine an area for growth and integrate strategies and actions with measurable goals for the school year. Alternatively, there could be different foci related to growth at each grade-level team with opportunities to share out goals and progress schoolwide. The work may also be incorporated into the overall school plan. Then teams could select different areas of growth that connect to what is being measured in the plan.

Common Questions

There are several questions that tend to arise when schools or districts first begin to implement the Young Scholars Model, reflecting some common assumptions and concerns about giftedness and talent development. Some of the most common questions and comments we have experienced are provided here, with possible responses:

> **Why should we single out these children?** Gifted programs and services exist to meet the diverse pathways of student development and ensure growth for every learner in an environment that typically tends to focus on grade-level proficiency and standardization. Yet for as long as gifted programs and advanced academic courses have been available, children from diverse cultural, linguistic, and economic backgrounds have been underrepresented. Educators must make every effort to find and nurture potential in all populations so that no child is denied access and no talent is left unactualized.

---

1 Note that the rubric provided in Figure 3 is primarily tailored for elementary-level implementation of the Young Scholars Model. An additional rubric more tailored to the secondary level appears in Chapter 8.

Figure 3
Young Scholars Model Implementation Rubric

	Launching	Developing	Highly Functioning
Committed Professionals	❧ The Young Scholars Model is seen primarily as the responsibility of one advocate (resource teacher, instructional coach, school-based administrator). ❧ Teachers are developing an understanding of the role of staff in the Young Scholars Model. ❧ A small number of program champions engage in data analysis and/or professional learning related to equity in gifted programs.	❧ School leaders are engaging in the Young Scholars Model, including the school leadership team, resource teacher or coach, and at least several staff in the school. ❧ All teachers are informed and participate in seeking and identifying young scholars. ❧ Some teachers are trying interventions with young scholars. ❧ Staff occasionally engage in conversation about culturally responsive teaching practices.	❧ The school leadership team, including the principal and coach, coordinate a strong and strategic Young Scholars Model in the school through a committee that ensures shared responsibility and leadership for model implementation. ❧ All teachers are informed, play a role in interventions, and feel personally committed to the support of young scholars in accessing advanced learning opportunities. ❧ Staff engage in frequent conversation and self-assessment regarding culturally responsive teaching practices.

Figure 3, *continued*

	Launching	Developing	Highly Functioning
Committed Professionals, *continued*		❧ School-based leaders engage in networking and professional learning efforts to deepen their understanding and ensure local measurement of what works (or doesn't) and why.	❧ School-based leaders engage in professional learning, measure what works (or doesn't) and why, and share their process, success, and challenges with other schools to build a network for continuous improvement.
Find and Identify	❧ One or two champions initiate most conversations about advocacy, affirmation, and access for learners. ❧ Staff are beginning to recognize the importance of context when talent scouting. ❧ Staff are familiar with or are becoming familiar with the principles of culturally responsive teaching (e.g., critical lens, voice and choice, rigor, perspective-taking).	❧ Staff are aware of and attend to the match between overall school demographics and students identified as young scholars and for gifted services. ❧ Staff are developing understanding of responses to high-level curriculum as an identification tool working hand in hand with culturally responsive teaching principles. ❧ Staff are developing understanding of the Young Scholars profile and supporting advocacy, affirmation, and access.	❧ Staff use data about the match of overall school demographics and students identified as young scholars and for gifted services as a tool for strengthening the implementation of the Young Scholars Model. ❧ Each grade level has strategic plans for frequent opportunities for young scholars' engagement with high-level curriculum as an identification tool working hand in hand with culturally responsive teaching principles. ❧ Staff regularly seek students who meet the Young Scholars profile. ❧ Portfolios are used to show student growth over time.

Figure 3, *continued*

	Launching	Developing	Highly Functioning
Nurture, Guide, and Support	❧ Young Scholars coding is not part of grouping considerations. ❧ Advanced curriculum is used but primarily by a resource teacher or only periodically by a classroom teacher (e.g., once per quarter).	❧ Young Scholars coding is part of grouping considerations at some grade levels. ❧ Curriculum use is shared by the resource teacher and by classroom teachers, and students have multiple opportunities each quarter to engage. ❧ Teachers are familiar with scaffolding strategies for access to high-level curriculum.	❧ Young scholars are cluster grouped at all grade levels with teachers who are committed to providing growth mindset culture and "teaching up" through high-level curriculum. ❧ Young scholars have weekly opportunities to work with high-level curriculum in the classroom. ❧ Teachers are skillful in using differentiation strategies for scaffolding or increasing rigor depending on student needs while engaging in high-level curriculum. ❧ The school offers extracurricular or supplemental opportunities for young scholars.

Figure 3, *continued*

Essential Elements	Launching	Developing	Highly Functioning
	❧ An overview of the Young Scholars Model is shared with staff and families. ❧ At least one schoolwide intervention is planned (curriculum, summer school, afterschool, family engagement, etc.).	❧ Multiple opportunities for professional learning to support the Young Scholars Model are offered for and attended by teachers. ❧ At least two schoolwide interventions are planned. ❧ Some vertical articulation is in place to ensure continued focus on the needs of identified young scholars. ❧ Schools seek some opportunities for family engagement beyond information about the Young Scholars Model.	❧ The resource teacher is part of professional learning community discussions and is able to support teachers in use of high-level curriculum as an intervention and talent-seeking measure. ❧ Classroom teachers at each grade level engage with professional learning on high-level curriculum. ❧ Planning for high-level curriculum experiences and student progress is embedded in the professional learning community process. ❧ Multiple strategic interventions are planned. ❧ School counselors are involved in vertical articulation of Young Scholars, from grade to grade and from elementary to middle to high school, to ensure continued focus on the needs of identified young scholars. ❧ Schools have a strategic plan and measured outcomes for family engagement.

❧ **We don't have any gifted kids in our school.** Historically, students have been identified for gifted programs through a reliance on ability and achievement test scores. Because some students may enter school with language learning needs, learning challenges, or gaps in "school knowledge," some school staff mistakenly believe that there is not advanced academic potential. To be clear, there are students with advanced learning needs in every population. In schools with more diverse populations, many students who have talents and academic strengths are never identified because their potential is not recognized through traditional measures. Using a variety of universal screeners—including responses to opportunities to use gifted strategies and curriculum or gifted rating scales built around culturally responsive principles—schools that implement the Young Scholars Model begin to find talent and advanced potential in places where they had not been looking. It is key to turn from *responding to talent* to *proactively providing opportunities that will reveal talent.*

❧ A parent of a child who does not fit the demographic profile of a young scholar may ask: **Why isn't my child a young scholar?** The principal or lead teacher may respond: You are your child's best advocate and are able to provide enrichment and extracurricular activities in order to develop and nurture their strengths. The families of young scholars require additional support to advocate for their student for a variety of reasons, such as language differences, economic struggles, or being new to U.S. education and having limited knowledge about gifted services. For young scholars, the school becomes their advocate to help provide access, affirmation, and opportunities to develop their talents and strengths.

❧ **Is Young Scholars just for students of color?** No, young scholars are students who show advanced thinking potential from any historically underrepresented populations, including children from diverse cultural, ethnic, linguistic, and economic backgrounds as well as twice-exceptional learners. The goal is to find students who show advanced thinking ability who may need school intervention for access, advocacy, and/or affirmation.

❧ **Can students participating in special education programs participate in the Young Scholars Model?** Yes, students who receive special education services can be identified as young scholars. The Young Scholars lead teacher collaborates with classroom teachers and special education teachers to identify young scholars and to determine the most appropriate way to serve them instructionally to show their strengths.

❧ **If a student is identified for gifted services, is Young Scholars still relevant?** Young Scholars is a complementary, wraparound service that helps to ensure success and guidance for students as they progress through their K–12 experience. If gifted services are available, initial identification of a young scholars should be coupled with immediate access to gifted services and/or advanced coursework. The Young Scholars label provides a safety net for students in that it will alert teachers that additional social-emotional or psychosocial supports may be helpful to ensure that students are successful and continue on a trajectory of enrollment in challenging coursework. Young Scholars is *not* a substitute to gifted services; it is a system of support that follows a student through their development from elementary to middle to high school that increases the likelihood that their potential can be actualized.

ও **How do you maintain high standards in advanced curriculum/courses with a broader identification framework? How do I know the curriculum is not "watered down"?** The curricula and resources that are used with Young Scholars, as well as formal gifted services, are research-based and designed for gifted learners. Nothing is watered down; however, teachers may provide additional scaffolds and supports as needed. Teachers are finding that over time and with appropriate support, young scholars are able to reach the same high standards and succeed in the same challenging learning experiences that are a hallmark of gifted pedagogy.

ও **Why are cluster grouping opportunities important for young scholars?** Providing opportunities to work on academic tasks with peers from a similar background provides students with a sense of belonging and safety when they are working on high-level tasks. Teachers support this belonging and safety by creating and/or selecting lessons that are both challenging and culturally relevant.

ও **Do these students *have* to get pull-out services? I have a young scholar in my class who is getting many other interventions, and I think it's more important that they are in the classroom so they don't miss core instruction.** School day, small-group interventions for these students should be driven by the collaboration between the Young Scholars teacher and the classroom teacher. Based on assessment data, this could be an extension and/or an opportunity to learn the core content in a different way, using targeted critical and creative thinking activities. This small-group intervention could happen after the Young Scholars teacher models a whole-class lesson for all students and/or coteaches a lesson with the classroom teacher and then has all students working in different groups within the classroom setting and/or in another setting.

If the Young Scholars lead teacher has opportunities to provide small-group enrichment opportunities before or after school, the content of these sessions could be more flexible in nature. This may provide an alternative venue for enrichment if the young scholars have demonstrated a need for core instruction.

> ❧ **Is Young Scholars just a summer program/just an afterschool program?** Young Scholars is designed as a comprehensive approach to supporting learners across multiple aspects of their academic growth, with attention to their learning experiences in the regular classroom as well as in enrichment experiences outside of the regular school day. Sometimes, a Young Scholars summer program may be the most visible aspect of the model, and it might be a major focus for a Young Scholars team starting out with implementation, but full implementation of the model is much more comprehensive.

> ❧ **Will all identified young scholars eventually be identified for gifted services?** Although the Young Scholars Model is a model of intervention designed to prepare students from historically underrepresented groups for success in advanced academic classes, not all young scholars will be formally identified for gifted programming.

If a school system has levels of service within gifted programming, the goal is for young scholars to be considered for a level of service in a minimum of one area of academic strength, if not multiple areas. As young scholars advance in grade level, early targeted supports create opportunities for affirmation of talent and the development of resiliency so that they will be prepared for more challenging coursework from elementary school to middle and high school. If the long-term goal is to prepare students for challenging coursework at the secondary level, front-loading opportunities and building a growth mindset are essential building blocks.

Tailoring the Model to the Context

In its first year of using the Young Scholars Model, several schools decided that the aspect of "maximizing the committed professionals" was a strategic place to begin. When self-assessing their school's current level of implementation against the rubric, they realized that the model was living almost wholly on the shoulders of the gifted resource teacher and that a vision for shared leadership with educators that reached further into school staff would be beneficial.

In one school, a collaboration between the assistant principal and gifted resource teacher resulted in bringing teachers together to form a Young Scholars committee that had broad representation from multiple teams across the school. Teacher representatives on the committee became notably invested in the mission of Young Scholars and became drivers to propel actions in other parts of the model. For example, several teachers enrolled in an afterschool course on strategies to engage advanced learners. They voluntarily stayed after school to learn about and implement ways to make student thinking visible. As the course progressed, the teachers took risks and scaffolded deeper learning experiences for students schoolwide. They also showcased their individualized construction of meaning from the course through exhibitions of learning from a practitioner perspective. Practices from this course were then shared with more teachers through collaborative learning teams, which were already meeting weekly. This committee also met to discuss how to continuously improve the model's implementation at their school.

The rapid growth that happened at this school was the result of shared leadership and an investment in the mission from teacher influencers in the building. This school shared about its success at Young Scholars principal networking meetings, and several other schools decided to implement a similar structure at their schools, built by their teachers and contextualized to their school structures and culture.

The principals and teachers at the Young Scholars schools are committed to increasing the number of learners from underserved populations receiving advanced academic services at their schools, and they play a key role in the success of this model. They view themselves as instructional leaders, and they meet several times a year with other school leaders to collaborate, share ideas, and tackle the challenges and concerns that must be addressed as they implement the model at their schools. These leaders are strong advocates for the students, and they ensure that year after year the young scholars are placed with teachers who know how to nurture and develop their advanced potential. A principal summed up the impact that participation in the program has had on her school staff:

> Anytime that you do something to look at a child's behavior or performance in a different way, then you're going to extend your perception of what's going on. So the more we look at children, the more we're going to find out about them. I think the more we work with Young Scholars, the more potential we're going to see. . . .

A teacher shared,

> Since I've worked with Young Scholars, my expectations have been broader; I have higher expectations for children who are able to perform better. Everyone has an idea of what giftedness is, but Young Scholars has broadened my perspective about who is brought into that category.

Entry Points and Growth Edges for Systemic Leadership

A strong Young Scholars Model may take shape from a grassroots effort, but the true power of the model depends on alignment and coherence. Figure 4 shows some sample indicators that may reveal entry points and growth edges around systemic leadership as an important component to Young Scholars Model implementation.

Figure 4
Indicators of Entry Points and Growth Edges for Systemic Leadership

Beginning Implementation	Developing Implementation	Deep Implementation and Monitoring for Improvement Areas
❧ Some leaders or teachers are focused on the power of the Young Scholars Model and make connections to overall district equity goals. ❧ There is awareness of the Young Scholars Model among staff, but actions do not yet align with goals.	❧ School-level leadership sets up the foundation for a school-level Young Scholars Model that is distributed across the school teams to provide a secure foundation that is not vulnerable to leadership changes or initiative fatigue. ❧ Goal setting and evaluation for measuring growth in components of the Young Scholars Model (committed professionals, find/identify, nurture/guide/support, essential elements) occurs on a periodic basis.	❧ Alignment is clear between district equity goals, messaging and support from district leadership, and networked implementation of the Young Scholars Model. ❧ School-level goal setting and growth are examined and reported to show growth in areas of model implementation; successful practices are connected to desired student outcomes so that continuous improvement is tied to results. ❧ Central office leaders collaborate with school instructional leaders with a focus on Young Scholars equity goals.

Chapter 3

Seeking and Identifying Potential in Young Scholars

> What educators and psychologists recognize as giftedness in children is really potential giftedness, which denotes promise rather than fulfillment and probabilities rather than certainties about future accomplishments. How high these probabilities are in any given case depends much upon the match between a child's budding talents and the kinds of nurturance provided.
>
> —A. Harry Passow

Identification of students in need of services is a central part of any programming designed to address exceptional needs. In gifted education, identification has long been both a central element of programming and a major point of contention. This contention results from varied definitions of giftedness, varied approaches to the identification process, and patterns of underrepresentation of specific populations in gifted programs.

Further, although identification is a necessary part of gifted programming for administrative and organizational purposes, it frequently leads to circumstances in which the process becomes more about getting a label than about access to needed services. Because Young Scholars is not a formal gifted identification process, teachers and school teams are encouraged to err on the side of inclusion. In the Young Scholars Model, nontraditional, holistic approaches to identification of students' needs for services are critical for successful implementation. These approaches include both the instructional tasks and assessments used and the involvement of many individuals.

We believe . . .

- ❧ Giftedness in children is potential, and how that potential is realized depends on the opportunities that students have to exhibit and develop their strengths.
- ❧ Identification is a process that supports access to gifted services; it is not a goal in itself but a means to designate the need for appropriate and advanced learning opportunities.
- ❧ Cultural values and norms influence how students exhibit their talents.
- ❧ Ability and achievement test scores may provide some evidence regarding potential but also carry multiple issues that may inadvertently cause some students to be overlooked; review of local building norms that consider but are not limited to test scores may be helpful in contextualizing student assessment data.
- ❧ Universal screening approaches facilitate finding overlooked potential, and early use of universal screening supports earlier access to Young Scholars services.
- ❧ Performance assessments and digital or paper portfolios help measure and record a student's growth over time and are essential elements in documenting the process of finding potential and determining appropriate supports.
- ❧ Professional learning opportunities are essential to support all school staff in scouting for talent with a strength-based focus rather than a deficit lens.

In this chapter . . .

- ❧ We describe multiple approaches that may be used to find and develop high academic potential in young scholars.
- ❧ We explain the role of learning tasks that require higher level thinking and high-end curriculum, both integral to the identification process.
- ❧ We provide suggestions for helping general education teachers think differently about behaviors that may be indicators of advanced potential.

Finding and supporting students with advanced potential from typically underserved populations is a central goal of the Young Scholars Model. Identification processes are foundational to the find/identify component of the model, but successful progress toward identification goals requires integration of all four elements:

Committed Professionals. Educators collaborate within the school community to find potential in students from backgrounds that have historically been overlooked. This effort requires professionals to examine where there may be barriers to access with current screening and identification procedures. It also requires examining the mindsets that may exist within school staff about the role of ability testing and the need to broaden the evidence used to identify students in a more holistic way.

Find and Identify. Effective identification processes within the Young Scholars Model ask two things of school staff members. First, the model asks teachers to examine their own beliefs about how talent is revealed to be sure they are not informed solely by their own perceptions, experiences, and cultural norms. Second, it asks teachers to provide opportunities through experiences with gifted pedagogy (e.g., instructional strategies, curriculum, authentic performance tasks) as a way to seek and identify talent.

Nurture, Guide, and Support. The model rests in part on educators' understanding of the importance of encouraging demonstration of talent potential among all students in learning environments that allow such potential to emerge. It asks teachers to provide ongoing opportunities for students to think critically and creatively with support. It also asks educators to capture evidence of talent and growth over time in response to these opportunities.

Essential Elements. Ongoing professional learning provides important support for identification processes because it promotes self-examination and equips educators with the strategies and tools needed to identify talent with nontraditional methods. Partnerships with families are critical because they guide communications and help parents and guardians understand effective ways to support and advocate for their child. Enrichment opportunities provide the young scholars with experiences in multiple fields of inquiry both during the school year and through summer school.

Gifted programs and services can be an important gateway for participation and success in challenging courses in high school and higher education. Therefore, implementation of the model must be guided by a belief in the importance of providing access to advanced learning opportunities to all students who have the potential to succeed. Young Scholars begins as a talent development initiative in a school or district. The goal is to give *all* students opportunities to demonstrate advanced potential early and often through learning experiences that present them with new learning challenges. Every student is encouraged to raise and exceed their own expectations and to participate in learning tasks that build on their strengths. Teachers are encouraged to err on the side of inclusion with the understanding that as potential emerges the students should be considered for any available gifted programs or advanced learning opportunities that the school offers.

The Young Scholars Model uses a comprehensive approach to find and nurture gifted potential with a special focus on students in historically underserved populations, such as students from diverse cultural, linguistic, and socioeconomic backgrounds, and twice-exceptional students. It does this by requiring schools to move beyond ability and achievement test scores and to employ a portfolio approach with documentation of student responses to challenging, thought-provoking learning tasks. Each Young Scholars school takes into consideration the diversity of background experiences that young learners bring to school and employs assessments and learning opportunities that capture students' potential in nontraditional ways.

Understanding Intelligence

The identification of talent potential must be grounded in an expanded understanding of intelligence that embraces diverse cultural, ethnic, and linguistic manifestations (Hodges et al., 2018). A narrow definition of intelligence that is measured by how well children perform on assessments that require a knowledge of words and numbers learned in school precludes participation in advanced academic programs for certain populations of students who have not had the opportunity to attain this knowledge before coming to school. This is critical, for it has major implications for the educational experiences that are provided to children. The shift from an understanding of intelligence as a static and innate ability grounded in a cultural and social context tied to Western, affluent populations to an understanding of intelligence as evolving potential that is contextually based and is nurtured through experience provides numerous possibilities for understanding giftedness as developing potential in a much broader range of students (Plucker & Peters, 2016).

The work of finding and nurturing young scholars is guided by an understanding that talent and intelligence:

- ❧ develop over time,
- ❧ can be nurtured,
- ❧ manifest in different ways in different cultures, and
- ❧ are complex and affected by both genetic and environmental influences.

Grounded in this epigenetic view of intelligence, identification systems become interdependent, with opportunity and focus increasingly on engaging students regularly with learning experiences that allow them to demonstrate potential, to access and respond to new challenges, and to show patterns of growth over time.

Changing demographics reinforce the need for assessments that are more equitable for students from diverse backgrounds. Research suggests that students from diverse backgrounds are underrepresented in gifted programs in public schools throughout the United States and that nontraditional methods have not adequately addressed this issue (Hodges et al., 2018).

From its inception, identification for gifted programming has often relied on group-administered ability tests that evaluate gifted potential in children by assessing their ability to think and reason through test items that require literacy and numeracy. Although standard ability tests do provide valuable information for many children, there are serious concerns about using them as a single data source when making judgments about a child's potential, especially for children who are affected by poverty, language, and/or special education needs (Pfeiffer, 2012). Traditional ability tests may fail to accurately evaluate advanced thinking and reasoning ability in students who do not have the verbal and mathematical knowledge and skills that are needed to successfully complete the items on these tests (Peters & Engerrand, 2016; Siegle et al., 2016; Smith et al., 1997). Although children from diverse cultural, economic, and linguistic backgrounds may have an advanced capacity to think, reason, and problem solve, these students may not appear to have differentiated learning needs without contextual considerations of the skills measured on ability tests that rely on learned verbal and mathematical skills but do not capture other indicators of advanced ability. Research suggests that tests that rely heavily on verbal and mathematical proficiency may eliminate students whose primary language is not English or students who have not had the opportunity to develop these skills before starting school (Brooks-Gunn et al., 1996; Sotelo-Dynega et al., 2013).

In addition, there are children who do exceptionally well on achievement tests even though their ability test scores are much lower, and other children who score well on ability tests whose achievement scores may not be commensurate with their assessed ability. Historically, traditional methods of identification have failed to find students from diverse cultural, economic, and linguistic backgrounds (Siegle et al., 2016). In addition to disparate opportunities for enrichment outside of school, there is also a need to be aware that some students have had extensive test preparation and may achieve high scores because the test has been practiced. All of these factors highlight the need for evidence from multiple measures and assessments as decisions are being made. Performance assessments that identify students across cultural, economic, and ethnic groups are a necessary component of the Young Scholars Model.

Approaches for Finding Young Scholars

Schools that implement the Young Scholars Model begin with engaging and challenging learning experiences with all students that can be used to collect evidence of children's interests, learning profiles, and strengths through observations, work samples, and anecdotal records. School professionals work together to find potential talent in young children through teaching and learning strategies designed to elicit higher level thinking. Instead of a focus on test scores and identifying who is gifted, the focus is on curriculum, its role as a major identifier of talent, and the interventions that are needed to develop that talent further. Lessons designed to teach students to think on a higher level accompanied by multidimensional assessments can increase the prospects of finding and nurturing talent in a broad range of learners.

Getting Started

A team implementing the Young Scholars Model is generally driven by an awareness of problems with access and equity within the school or district population. The model is a response to a need for greater access to advanced learning for children who would benefit from those experiences and who come from populations traditionally underserved by advanced learning programs. Starting from that sense of a need for greater equity, the team can begin with examining the actual data about access to gifted and advanced learning programs, using guiding questions such as the following:

❧ Of your students who are receiving free and reduced price lunch, what percentage are being identified for gifted services?

❧ What percentage of your English language learners are being identified for gifted services?

❧ What percentage of students from historically underrepresented groups, including Black, Hispanic, and Native American students, are being identified for gifted services?

❧ To what degree do the demographics of your identified gifted population mirror the overall demographics of the school?

❧ If the identification system includes multiple steps of screening and review, at what stages are students from underrepresented groups disappearing from the pool of candidates for gifted services?

This kind of review of the data can demonstrate where there are likely students going unnoticed for opportunities for advanced learning. It also provides context for the team supporting young scholars, and potentially the wider staff of the school, to have conversations about assumptions about talent development and about talent potential and its existence in all populations served by the school.

Finding and Identifying Young Scholars

Young Scholars is separate from a district's program for gifted services. It is a model for finding and supporting children who show advanced potential compared to students of similar age, background, and experience, but who may have special challenges presented by their circumstances. Identification as a young scholar often provides the additional support these students need for access to and success in advanced learning programs, including early intervention efforts, enrichment experiences, and wraparound services throughout students' K–12 school life. Many young scholars are identified for formal gifted services, but it is not a requirement; the focus is on curriculum, its role as a major identifier of talent, and the services that are needed to develop that talent. Teachers are encouraged to err on the side of inclusion because Young Scholars is an important path for accessing a variety of advanced learning opportunities, whatever the official identification process for gifted services may be. The checklist in Figure 5 may be a helpful guide as schools begin to search for talent and implement the model.

The model is grounded in an expanded understanding of intelligence that embraces diverse cultural, ethnic, and linguistic manifestations of talent. New and innovative assessments are needed to identify students who demonstrate excep-

Figure 5
Implementation Checklist for Identification of Young Scholars

Nontraditional Methods of Nurturing and Developing Talent				
	Level of Implementation			
	Low			High
Gifted education strategies and practices are infused into the general education curriculum for all learners to elicit and identify gifted behaviors and academic strengths.				
Beginning in kindergarten, the school offers a continuum of gifted services with multiple entry points and varying levels of challenge in response to ongoing assessments in reading and mathematics.				
Teachers record evidence of gifted potential through portfolios. Evidence is collected in response to thinking strategy instruction and includes observations, work samples, performance assessments, anecdotal records, and test scores.				
Advanced curriculum and instruction are available to any child who has the capacity to succeed as determined through performance assessments and multiple criteria.				
As young scholars are identified, the students receive a "YS" designation in the student data system, which also records the type of service each student receives, when the service began, and the subject area(s) in which the student receives advanced instruction.				
Summer school, as well as before- and afterschool opportunities, provide ongoing enrichment and acceleration in one or more academic areas.				

Figure 5, *continued*

Nontraditional Methods of Nurturing and Developing Talent
Strengths:
Goals for Improvement (to include professional learning needs):

tional potential in a broad range of domains. As current theories suggest, if intelligence is a multifaceted and multidimensional potential that is ever-evolving in response to internal and external catalysts, then educators have an active role to play in searching for potential talent among students of varying cultural, ethnic, and linguistic backgrounds to provide an educational setting that will identify and nurture that potential (Nisbett et al., 2012).

Part of the Young Scholars Model involves setting up a system in the school for noticing, seeking, and finding children who show potential to benefit from advanced learning experiences, again in comparison to other students of similar age, background, and experiences. This system should include ongoing processes whereby any school staff member may bring a child to the attention of the Young Scholars team. The system also involves active, classroom-based activities with all learners designed to draw out behaviors that might be indicative of advanced potential. Such activities can be conducted by classroom teachers, preferably in collaboration with a resource teacher who can support classroom teachers in observing and documenting student behaviors in response to challenging tasks. This talent scouting is a critical and ongoing part of identifying potential, or signs that student abilities may fall outside of the norm compared to students of similar age, background, and experiences. In the words of one teacher:

> I have a little girl in kindergarten who is quiet and yet is a very intense thinker. She made a comment one time when we were talking about letters and sounds. She asked if things had to be in

order. She asked if things in math had to be in order, as letters have to be in order to make a word.

If the school does not have a gifted resource teacher, then a teacher leader is selected to act as an advocate for the students and a guide in the process of observing and noticing behaviors to identify young scholars. Preferably, the teacher leader has an endorsement in gifted education or has engaged in professional learning activities with a focus on advanced learners in historically underserved populations. This could be an equity resource teacher or someone who has a strong background in culturally responsive teaching and a focus on gifted learners.

Through the systematic observation of all students, a collection of anecdotal records, and a careful review of portfolios of student work samples, beginning in kindergarten, classroom teachers identify and nurture students who have gifted potential (i.e., an ability to think, reason, and problem solve at a level that is advanced in comparison to their peers of similar age, background, and experience). Although it is important to find young scholars as early as possible, they may be identified and coded at any grade level.

Voices From the Field

Using nontraditional methods of identification is critical to ensuring that young scholars are identified for advanced academic services. Using work samples and teacher input has helped to provide a holistic picture of our students' strengths. The focus on students' strengths through nontraditional methods of identification enables us to identify and nurture student potential of our young scholars that may have been missed if solely focused on test scores.

This past school year, a student was identified for full-time advanced academic services starting in fourth grade. This student was new to the country at the end of April during her second-grade year. While she only spoke Spanish when she arrived at our school, her teacher recognized that she was acquiring language at a rapid pace and was extremely curious. With scaffolds put into place in collaboration with the English language teacher, the student was able to understand tasks and complete assignments with limited English. Because she was provided with access to authentic, rigorous learning experiences with proper scaffolds, we quickly saw this student's potential through her work samples and daily interactions. At the end of second grade, this student was identified as a young scholar.

In third grade, this student flourished and was quickly identified for part-time advanced academic services. Her teacher collaborated with me and the English language teacher to ensure that she was differentiating for this student across content areas while providing scaffolds to support her development with the English language. While the student receives Limited English Proficiency Level I services, she is able to process content and make strong connections at a rate faster than her peers. When the student took an ability test in third grade, she had scores that were below average or average. Her potential was not recognized through this assessment. Her work samples and observable behaviors, however, showed that she has an exceptional ability to learn, demonstrates exceptional application of knowledge, has exceptional creative thinking abilities, and has an exceptional motivation to succeed. Using nontraditional methods of identification helped us recognize this student's potential so that we could nurture that potential. With this support, she is going to begin receiving full-time advanced academic services in fourth grade. If we had focused solely on the traditional methods of identification, we may have missed the potential of not only this student, but also many other young scholars.

—Jamie Wilson, Advanced Academic Resource Teacher

Using Critical and Creative Thinking to Elicit and Identify Exceptional Talents and Strengths

As part of a strong talent development program, frequent opportunities should be afforded to all students to engage in challenging learning activities that invite them to demonstrate critical and creative thinking. Such learning activities provide an important context for seeking talent potential, particularly because they provide the space to consider student responses compared to other students of similar age, background, and experience. Although the embrace of 21st-century skills over the last 2 decades has somewhat increased the likelihood of higher level thinking opportunities in more classrooms, there still exists a pattern, termed a "pedagogy of poverty," whereby a deficit model intended to prepare students for a standardized test takes priority over strategies and curriculum that unleash student engagement and reveal talent (Haberman, 2010). It is important to ensure that higher level instructional opportunities are frequently woven into student experiences. These may emerge from a school- or districtwide critical and creative thinking framework or a resource written for advanced learners; either way, student experiences should provide them opportunities to show not just what they know, but how they think. Such a framework might identify specific thinking emphases that should be infused across content areas and grade levels, with guidelines and resources for teachers to use to support this infusion.

For example, Figure 6 explains a set of nine strategies with examples of how they might be employed in talent seeking. Having such a common set of strategies to support higher level thinking enables schools to have common language and entry points for all teachers and students to this effort. Further practical applications for several of these strategies may be found in the Appendix.

In another example, Figure 7 shows similar emphases organized around broad goals for instruction to support student development of thinking and reasoning. Several sample instructional strategies connected with each goal are identified to provide guidance for teachers in their efforts to support talent seeking and talent development.

Such frameworks are the starting place for helping teachers and students engage with higher level thinking behaviors across content areas and grade levels, with a common vocabulary and shared understanding of how the strategies work. If a district does not have such a framework in place, you might start with the examples in Figures 6 and 7. Another useful resource is the "Thinking Routine Toolbox" from Harvard's Project Zero. This emerged from years of different research projects related to using and encouraging thinking strategies (see http://www.pz.harvard.edu/thinking-routines; also Ritchhart & Church, 2020). The toolbox specifies some core thinking routines, with emphasis on asking questions, making connections, and exploring perspectives; it also provides a wide range of additional resources around aspects of exploring and clarifying ideas and perspectives in depth.

Classroom teachers can introduce these thinking strategies as stand-alone activities, or they may integrate them into subject-area lessons. The strategies increase student engagement and provide opportunities for a higher level of thinking than may be found in typical lessons. Students are taught the name of the strategy and how it can help them become better thinkers. They are also given opportunities to apply the thinking strategies in different content areas. The strategies become part of a toolbox for both teachers and students.

Active guidance for the development of thinking skills allows children to become actively engaged in their learning, increases their independence, and helps them develop their talents and potential. Thinking, reasoning, reflecting, analyzing, discussing, and applying new ideas are essential characteristics of a climate of learning that encourages students to think on a higher level, challenge existing ideas, and entertain new possibilities for the future. Critical and creative thinking strategies encourage students to move beyond a focus on getting the right answer for a test and instead encourage them to question the answers, formulate their

Figure 6
Sample Critical and Creative Thinking Strategies

Questioning

Active learners are always questioning. Learning to ask and answer good questions is an important skill that nurtures inquiring minds. When students engage in learning activities that deliberately provide the space and support for asking questions, particularly when these activities help students go beyond brief, fact-based questions, they are taking a more dynamic approach to learning that stimulates reflection and inquiry. Teachers model different approaches to questioning, including using essential questions to guide learning, posing reflective and self-evaluative questions, and developing questions to deepen understanding. They also provide specific tasks that engage students in asking questions; note that "questioning" as a critical and creative thinking strategy refers primarily to *students* as they ask questions, not teachers (except for modeling purposes).

Observing and documenting student questions can be an important way of recognizing potential. What types of questions do students ask? When do they ask questions to clarify understanding, seek another perspective, explore connections, or pursue depth in learning? Which students demonstrate metacognition in how they question and evaluate their own work or next steps? Questioning is an important strategy that teaches students to clarify, explore, challenge, and assess their understanding of content and ideas; it is also evidence of how students think as they approach new learning experiences.

Fluency, Originality, Flexibility, and Elaboration

Fluency, originality, flexibility, and elaboration represent parts of creative thinking, particularly divergent thinking. Tasks that call for fluency and flexibility open up the thinking of students to consider many possibilities by encouraging the generation of many ideas and thinking of how to use ideas in different ways. A focus on originality and elaboration stretches the uniqueness and depth of students' thinking with attention to new and different ideas and the ability to explain ideas in greater depth. Using this strategy instructionally invites students to generate and explore ideas, and it provides space for students to show creative thinking and curiosity among other behaviors that may indicate high potential. When applied as a step in problem solving, the strategy also helps to show students' perceptiveness and strategic thinking as they generate ideas and then evaluate them in context.

Figure 6, *continued*

Visualization

This strategy opens up student thinking by using words, images, and/or simulated experiences to stimulate the imagination. It promotes students' abstract thinking by engaging them in the visualization of things that are not physically present. The process of visualization can also help students plan out an experience before execution. It allows students to set goals, visualize the steps they need to take to achieve them, and decide how to handle potential roadblocks before encountering them, which can build resiliency and increase organization. Visualization also increases the level and depth of comprehension of both spoken and written words. When students are engaged in visualization and encouraged to communicate about their thinking, teachers can observe aspects of student perceptiveness, their creative thinking, and the logic and organization they bring to their thinking. The strategy also provides space for teachers to observe the level of detail students are able to bring to their thinking and how they are able to communicate and elaborate on those details.

Mind Mapping

Mind mapping is a strategy for visual note-taking that helps students organize information in unique and personal ways. It allows students to build and see a whole picture at once and make connections among related ideas without interruption. Students begin by writing or drawing a main idea, subject, or concept in the center of the page. They then use lines to add symbols, words, colors, and/or images representing subtopics that connect to the main idea; then as the map grows, other ideas and details can branch out from these. This thinking skill encourages students' visual thinking and ability to make connections among ideas. It can also serve as a useful preassessment about students' background knowledge, and a postassessment to demonstrate what they have learned. Mind mapping gives students an understanding of the breadth of a topic, and it can help them narrow down their questions or research to one or more specific areas. As they map out their thinking, they are better able to identify connections among related ideas. The process of creating a mind map helps them understand, retain, remember, and recall information. Although the ideas and information illustrated may be similar, each mind map is an individual creation, displaying a student's understanding of connections, ability to organize ideas, and ways of communicating their thinking.

Figure 6, *continued*

Point of View

This thinking strategy allows students to explore an idea from multiple perspectives. It helps to broaden students' thinking and demonstrates that an idea should be examined from many points of view before an opinion is formed. The discipline of examining an issue from many perspectives will provide students with a good model for open-ended receptive thinking and empathizing with the opinions of others. It is important for children to become comfortable sharing their own viewpoints as they listen to and learn from others, and for them to understand the types of dialogue and discussion that support healthy sharing of different points of view. When teachers engage students in this strategy, they can observe students' ability to recognize and understand different perspectives, engage productively in both speaking and listening as part of a dialogue, and explore relationships between points of view and the beliefs and evidence sources connected to them.

Analogies

Innovation and creative thinking are valuable skills that are needed in today's workforce. Analogies are a powerful thinking tool because they build upon the brain's natural inclination to make comparisons, draw connections, and see new possibilities. Analogies not only stimulate the imagination, but also lead children to deeper understandings by connecting things that do not always appear connected. Once students understand how analogies work, there are numerous questions and sentence starters that may be used to stimulate the imagination and lead them to deeper understandings by connecting things that do not always appear connected. Analogies also enhance flexible thinking and encourage students to make connections at a more sophisticated level. A facility for working with analogies gives students a structure for generating creative ideas, seeing complex relationships, and making unusual comparisons. When teachers employ analogies as a strategy, they have multiple opportunities to see the kinds of connections that students are able to draw and how those connections demonstrate capacity for flexibility in thinking, understanding abstraction, and seeing patterns and relationships.

Figure 6, *continued*

Encapsulation

Encapsulation is the process of pulling together the essence of an idea or situation and stating it in a concise, precise form. It is not simply stating the main idea or restating information or opinions. Encapsulation requires students to synthesize information and nuances to capture what is most important about an idea, object, or activity, and then communicate their thoughts clearly. It is the art of sharing ideas or information as succinctly as possible to get to "the bottom line" or the heart of a story, experience, or other information. Encapsulation requires that the student use as few words as possible and at the same time not lose the intention or scope of the original idea. For example, a teacher might ask students to describe a novel, event, or situation in three words. Or students may be asked to create a tweet or a license plate that encapsulates their understanding of an issue or idea. Another example is to ask students to underline salient points as they read a scientific article or an historical document and then use just a few of those words to encapsulate the reading. As students learn to encapsulate what they learn, they strengthen their confidence to express ideas in their own words. When teachers employ encapsulation as a strategy, they are encouraging students to engage in synthesis and to demonstrate their capacity for understanding big ideas, prioritizing key messages, and communicating critical information.

Decisions and Outcomes

Decision making is integral to everything we do. Helping students learn and understand the thinking processes that lead to good decisions is an important skill that will serve them well now and in the future. This thinking strategy provides a framework in which students can assess and evaluate a variety of decisions and possible outcomes. Understanding cause-and-effect relationships helps students recognize the importance of examining the outcomes of multiple decision options before embarking on a course of action. The concept of examining outcomes is relevant for all students as they learn to consider both short-term and long-range consequences in the decision-making process. Student responses may provide powerful evidence of their ability to understand and apply this important thinking skill.

Figure 6, *continued*

Plus, Minus, Interesting (PMI)

The PMI strategy encourages students to think about many possibilities and to explore the positive and negative aspects of ideas or situations. PMI encourages students to develop the habit of looking beyond the polarity of "yes or no," "wrong or right," and "my answer or your answer." The goal of PMI is to develop independent thinkers who consider a range of ideas and/or possibilities and see beyond the obvious. The plus category is for positive aspects, or "pros" that could be considered; the minus category is for negative aspects, or "cons" to be considered. The interesting category may include neutral thoughts and ideas, additional considerations, and questions. This strategy works well when discussing books, articles, field trips, current events, or any other ideas that can be considered through the lens of plus, minus, and interesting aspects. Often the interesting column leads to deeper insights and an understanding of the nuances inherent in each situation, event, or decision-making process. When teachers employ the PMI strategy, they are able to observe students' ability to consider multiple perspectives, recognize patterns, and predict possible outcomes. Students also show their capacity to evaluate circumstances and communicate their thinking.

own ideas, and seek solutions that are not ordinarily considered. Such strategies may be used at all grade levels and in all content areas. They provide multiple opportunities for students to explore knowledge, gain understanding, and acquire skills in work that stimulates minds and develops unique talents.

Critical and creative thinking strategies, when actively and consistently employed, provide support for all learners. They also provide an important context for recognizing talent potential. As teachers implement such strategies, they observe how students respond to the lessons, with a focus on how quickly, creatively, and proficiently students are able to approach new content and employ the strategies. Teachers then keep notes on student behaviors and products in these learning contexts, particularly with a focus on learners from underserved populations, as indicators of potential needs for more advanced learning opportunities through the Young Scholars Model.

Teachers who embed these strategies into instruction will lay the foundation for developing better thinkers while they are looking for and recognizing potential in students who may not otherwise have the opportunity to demonstrate their advanced thinking. When students are challenged through learning experiences

Figure 7
Framework and Examples for Supporting
Critical and Creative Thinking Instruction

Big Ideas
✎ Overarching concepts (change, systems, perspectives)
✎ Encapsulation
Critical Thinking Models
✎ Center for Gifted Education thinking models
✎ Project Zero thinking routines
Creative Thinking Approaches
✎ Fluency, flexibility, originality, elaboration (FFOE)
✎ SCAMPER
Decisions and Outcomes
✎ Plus, minus, interesting (PMI)
✎ Visualization
Making Connections
✎ Analogies
✎ Mind mapping
Point of View/Perspective
✎ de Bono's Hats
✎ Persuasion and debate
Questioning
✎ Socratic seminar
✎ Question Formulation Technique (QFT)

that require advanced applications of knowledge, they are motivated to reach new heights and move beyond existing limitations. Equity of opportunity becomes a reality when every student is encouraged to raise and exceed their own expectations through learning experiences that challenge them to discover and develop their highest potential.

Voices From the Field

My district is an underfunded urban setting. The [critical and creative thinking] lessons allowed students opportunities to learn, grow, and thrive that normally would not be available to them. Lessons were designed to engage students in hands-on ways, where they internalize their learning and share it out. Students were given the opportunity to discover in unique/nontraditional ways. The lessons truly helped me understand certain students in a different way. This ultimately helped me become a stronger educator, focused on the strengths of each individual. High-potential behaviors were unveiled, and strengths were brought to light that I was never aware of or looking for before going through the program.
—Rachel B., Young Scholars classroom teacher

Whether a school district has a formal gifted program, enrichment opportunities for all students, or advanced learning in specific subject areas, the goal of Young Scholars is to ensure that students who have historically lacked access to these opportunities are included. The school becomes their advocate, and educators work with parents/guardians to either inform and guide families through the identification process or to encourage student participation in the enrichment and advanced learning opportunities that are available. Teachers and other staff challenge all students through learning tasks that require higher level thinking and problem solving. They observe behaviors that demonstrate a need and readiness for additional intellectual challenge and collect evidence of potential talent that can be nurtured and developed.

Engaging Teachers in Conversation About Exceptional Talent in Diverse Populations

At its inception, Young Scholars started with dialogue, and the model continues to grow through powerful conversations. Conversations among administrators, teachers, and specialists ignite questions and generate discussions that lead to new ways of finding and nurturing gifted potential in diverse populations of learners. As one teacher recently commented,

> I think there are a lot of kids who aren't really identified because they are not as verbal as others. And sometimes the verbal ones that do like to talk a lot are not as gifted as some of the other ones who are the quiet thinkers and who come up with really outstanding answers.

Teachers at the Young Scholars schools engage extensively in professional learning and professional conversations to support their understanding of how important it is to take into consideration the diversity of background experiences that the young scholars bring. They learn instructional strategies designed to elicit high-level responses and ways to record evidence of gifted potential through observations, anecdotal records, and portfolios of student work. For example, the gifted and talented resource teacher or teacher leader may model a lesson on creating analogies while the classroom teacher observes and records student responses and behaviors. Next, the classroom teacher will conduct a lesson while the gifted and talented resource teacher or teacher leader records. Ensuing conversations between the gifted and talented resource teacher or teacher leader and the classroom teacher help expand everyone's understanding of gifted potential as they discuss observations and identify advanced learners who are at risk of not being identified.

Ongoing assessments by educators who have been trained to provide curriculum and instruction that are designed to elicit gifted behaviors may be the most powerful means of identifying advanced learners in historically underrepresented populations. As one teacher recently stated,

> I have discovered that there are many methods one can utilize to identify giftedness other than merely relying on standardized test results. I am now a strong supporter of portfolio presentations and anecdotal records to illustrate a child's strengths and talents.

Timeline for Identifying Young Scholars

September/October

- ❧ Begin by introducing the whole school staff to the Young Scholars Model through a staff meeting or grade-level team meetings (specialists and support staff should be included). Be sure to allow time and support for staff to make connections to existing equity initiatives so that they can see how Young Scholars fits into the bigger picture. Encourage follow-up conversations among staff to continue developing understanding of the model and the talent seeking and talent development goals it addresses. Highlight the following important information:

- ❧ Young scholars are students from historically underserved populations. This may include students with diverse cultural, linguistic, and economic backgrounds who are at risk of not being identified by traditional methods for advanced academic services. It also might include twice-exceptional students whose abilities may be masked or for whom a school may traditionally focus more on deficits rather than strengths. Students from these groups have been historically and consistently overlooked for many advanced academic programs.

- ❧ The Young Scholars Model provides *access* to resources and experiences that nurture gifted potential, *affirmation* of their potential to develop their self-efficacy, and *advocates* who ensure that their potential is recognized and developed.

- ❧ The screening process is more flexible than formal screening for gifted identification and errs on the side of inclusion. A combination of test scores, anecdotal records, portfolios, and work samples that demonstrate an ability to think, reason, and problem solve on an advanced level are collected in a student portfolio.

- ❧ Screening takes place in all grade levels beginning in kindergarten. The first meeting will occur after classroom teachers have had time to review general information about the Young Scholars Model and plans for implementation.

- ❧ Explain that there will be an ongoing discussion about the students. Teachers should use a file folder to keep anecdotal notes and work samples as students demonstrate high potential in one or more areas.

- ❧ After classroom teachers have had the opportunity to get to know their students and understand the model, they may begin to establish a list of students to *be considered as* young scholars and collect data on those individuals. The data may be kept in an online portfolio or a file folder to be used as evidence during the selection process.

November/December

- ⊷ Work samples highlighting student strengths are collected in a portfolio, either in a folder or online. Work may come from lessons that use strategies or curriculum designed for advanced learners, as this will allow students to demonstrate gifted behaviors through the open-ended, divergent, or problem-solving types of opportunities they provide.
- ⊷ Grade-level teams meet to revise a list of potential young scholars based on portfolios and classroom assessments.
- ⊷ Teachers take time to review the documents, ask questions, and gain clarification before evaluating their students.
- ⊷ Throughout all of these efforts, the team should be continuing to provide services for previously identified young scholars and continuing to provide classroom teachers with resources and ideas for supporting talent development in current young scholars.

February/March/April

- ⊷ School staff continue working with identified young scholars and encouraging teachers to refer additional students who are demonstrating evidence of advanced academic potential in their classrooms.
- ⊷ New students in grades K–6 who have recently entered the school may be screened at any time.
- ⊷ Each young scholar has a "YS" code in the school's database to facilitate record-keeping and ongoing support.
- ⊷ The school team plans and prepares to invite students to the Young Scholars summer school program (if you are offering summer school).

When a district establishes Young Scholars as an approach, part of the documentation system should include ensuring that students identified for Young Scholars receive a YS code in the student information system. This code stays with them through graduation from high school. It is separate from any gifted identification code and will allow the district to document Young Scholars participation and conduct longitudinal studies on the effectiveness of the model. For example, evaluation of the model in practice may include documenting such information as how many young scholars receive gifted services, participate in Advanced Placement courses, earn an International Baccalaureate diploma, and/ or go on to higher education. These data then become an important record of the success of the model. The YS code is also an important identifier of students who need advocacy and support from the school district as they transition to middle and high school. Overall, the model carries a strong emphasis on identification as a vehicle for access to services and a focus on the types of services students receive as opposed to labeling students.

As students engage in learning experiences that require advanced applications of knowledge, they discover and develop their own strengths and talents. Instructional strategies that require and promote higher level thinking provide myriad opportunities for students to explore knowledge, gain understanding, and acquire skills in work that stimulates their minds and develops their potential. They also provide observable evidence of a student's ability to think and reason at advanced levels (Horn, 2018; Robinson et al., 2018; VanTassel-Baska et al., 2002). Student performance on tasks that require critical and creative thinking and advanced problem solving provides powerful evidence of a student's gifted potential. In the Young Scholars Model, early identification of academic strengths and talents coupled with early interventions allows the school to provide the appropriate level of challenge and increase the students' self-efficacy. The long-term goal is for young scholars to participate and succeed in gifted programs or advanced academic courses as they discover and develop their strengths and talents.

Entry Points and Growth Edges
for Identification Practices

A strong Young Scholars Model may take shape from a grassroots effort, but the true power of the model depends on systemic alignment and coherence. Figure 8 shows some sample indicators that may reveal entry points and growth edges around identification of young scholars as an important component to Young Scholars Model implementation.

Figure 8
*Indicators of Entry Points and Growth Edges
for Identification of Young Scholars*

Beginning Implementation	Developing Implementation	Deep Implementation and Monitoring for Improvement Areas
≈ Universal screeners ensure all students are considered. ≈ Instructional leaders in the school ensure frequent opportunities in each class for student interest and talent to be revealed. This may involve strong support of a gifted resource teacher or instructional coach with expertise in strategies or curriculum for gifted students.	≈ Universal screeners go beyond ability tests (e.g., consider work samples and gifted behaviors scales). ≈ Universal screeners consider students in comparison to students of similar age, background, and experience. ≈ Instructional leaders in the school ensure frequent opportunities in each class for student interest and talent to be revealed. Teachers are responsible for delivery of instructional opportunities with minimal support of instructional coach with expertise.	≈ Robust universal screeners prompt teacher dialogue for identifying students with a Young Scholars profile multiple times per year. ≈ Frequent opportunities to use gifted curriculum in a variety of content areas demonstrate continuous pathways for talent development that are provided by every classroom teacher. ≈ Instructional coach with expertise in gifted strategies and curriculum documents observations about student strengths and growth, including transition conversations from grade to grade or from elementary to middle to high school.

Chapter 4

High-Quality Curriculum

> To the degree that deeper learning remains unavailable to students of color and children of low-income families, America will never be able to solve its equity dilemma. (Noguera et al., 2015)

High-quality curriculum and instruction are an important part of the Young Scholars Model. Access to challenging and rigorous learning experiences is central to talent development, and such experiences also build students' readiness to manage increasingly challenging academic tasks. Teachers with a solid understanding of the curriculum and effective instructional strategies facilitate and nurture talent development in all populations of students.

In Young Scholars schools, curriculum forms part of the *talent-spotting* aspect of the model as well as the *talent development* aspect of the model. All students have access to high-quality, challenging curricular experiences that invite higher level thinking. Teachers and specialists observe how students interact with the curriculum and provide additional scaffolding, support, and challenge opportunities for students who show a need for ongoing advanced learning. For students designated as young scholars, targeted interventions and learning opportunities during school and outside of school incorporate rigorous, high-quality curriculum as a way to build self-efficacy, encourage intellectual growth, and equip students with the tools they will need to be successful in advanced learning experiences as they move up in grade level.

We believe . . .

- ❧ Curriculum that is planned and written down within an organizing and rigorous framework supports and facilitates student engagement.
- ❧ Curricular units designed to give students a comprehensive experience, rather than episodic or stand-alone lessons or activities, bring deeper value to student learning and understanding.
- ❧ Teaching models designed around higher level thinking provide support to students as they work with challenging questions and problems. Units that promote challenge and high levels of engagement will prepare students for benchmark measures of grade-level proficiency while also developing thinking skills that will transfer and serve the student beyond standardized testing.
- ❧ Curriculum and instruction that emphasize rigor and challenge while embedding opportunities for support and scaffolding promote student growth and learning.
- ❧ Curriculum serves as a vehicle for talent spotting as well as for talent development.
- ❧ High-quality curriculum incorporates space for teachers to implement with fidelity as well as exercise professional judgment and make informed choices about the learning experiences of the students in their classes.
- ❧ Curriculum and instruction that incorporate choices for learners promote student ownership and motivation for learning.
- ❧ Curriculum and instruction designed around conceptual learning and understanding facilitate interdisciplinary connections.
- ❧ Successful school districts value and facilitate collaboration among content offices; program offices, such as gifted services, multitiered systems of support, arts, special education, English language learners, and family engagement; and school staff. Such collaboration supports consistent language, curriculum design, and vision for talent development through the use of recommended interventions and resources.

In this chapter . . .

ﾠ We explore defining features of high-quality curriculum designed for advanced learners.

ﾠ We discuss ways of using curriculum for talent spotting as well as for supporting talent development.

ﾠ We demonstrate how high-level curriculum and instruction may be integrated into the Young Scholars implementation plan.

The emphasis on high-quality curriculum connects to all four parts of the Young Scholars Model:

Committed Professionals. Teachers and instructional leaders must broaden their repertoire and vision of classroom practice for all students to include strategies and curriculum that may have been traditionally reserved for students identified for gifted services.

Find and Identify. Educators working in the Young Scholars Model maintain a focus on seeking talent. Such a focus includes the choice to implement advanced curriculum materials as an instrument for looking for talent and not just serving it. This implies using advanced curriculum with all learners to create an environment in which students show thinking processes and/or problem-solving approaches that may not emerge with more traditional lesson structures or assessments.

Nurture, Guide, and Support. As students reveal behaviors indicating high potential, educators continue to nurture and support their talents through access to and scaffolding for success with high-quality curriculum.

Essential Elements. District and school leaders must examine how the elements of high-quality curriculum are embedded in professional learning for teachers. Further, they must consider how to close gaps in access through curricular experiences in afterschool or summer enrichment programs that may not be accessible to young scholars without school support and advocacy.

Features of High-Quality Curriculum

We define high-quality curriculum for Young Scholars as that which allows students to access learning experiences that are rigorous, comprehensive, relevant, and engaging while promoting their individual growth. High-quality curriculum also requires attention to culturally responsive and representative content and teaching practices. The curriculum must be appropriate and challenging for the discipline under study, with emphasis on instructional activities that provide support for student access as well as space to extend and advance learning.

In some instances, the curriculum for Young Scholars may include resources that were specifically designed for an advanced learner population. For example, the K–3 science units that were developed as part of Project Clarion by the Center for Gifted Education at William & Mary fall into this category (Kim et al., 2012). In other instances, the resources are designed for a general education population but incorporate tasks that require higher level thinking and provide appropriate space for challenge for advanced learners; an example of these would be document-based question (DBQ) units in social studies (see https://dbqproj ect.com).

Curriculum should be rigorous, comprehensive, relevant and representative, and engaging.

Rigorous

Rigor in high-quality curriculum includes emphasis on goals and objectives that are central to the discipline under study and challenging for the students who are engaged with those goals and objectives. Such curriculum should incorporate high expectations for student engagement with the practices of the disciplines, deep thinking about central concepts, and supported exposure to advanced content. Rigor means that the curriculum engages learners in work that leads to an understanding of the concepts and principles at the heart of a discipline, as well as a thorough investigation of how concepts emerge in similar and different ways across the subjects under study. This kind of depth in the curriculum provides multiple opportunities for students to show their ability to focus on big ideas, recognize patterns and connections, and engage with abstract thinking.

Rigor also means that the curricular materials invite students to wrestle with questions that do not have easy or straightforward answers, and to incorporate multiple perspectives into their thinking about issues and problems. Such emphasis on complexity of perspective and no quick paths to right answers provides the space for students to demonstrate how they are learning to engage their critical thinking in response to problems and issues.

This emphasis on rigor should not limit access. High-quality curriculum should provide points of entry and scaffolds to allow learners from a wide range of backgrounds and experiences to engage with the learning. For example, educators should seek tasks and questions that have broad relevance and allow students to wrestle with big ideas while drawing on a wide range of background experiences, rather than linking to a *specific* experience that some students may not have had. Such points of entry and scaffolds are intended to broaden access. When teachers implement rigorous curriculum materials that provide a wide range of space for student response and engagement, students have more opportunities to show what they can do.

An additional aspect of rigor that is a consideration for high-quality curriculum is the inclusion of an assessment system that supports a clear alignment of intended learning outcomes, learning activities, and assessment strategies. The curriculum materials should provide guidelines and resources for teachers around assessment, and the assessment strategies should provide sufficient ceiling to allow students capable of advanced work to show the scope of their learning.

Comprehensive

Curriculum is more supportive of deep learning and growth for students when it is organized into comprehensive units that integrate multiple standards, skills, and depth of content. Sometimes, approaches to instruction involve stand-alone activities or abbreviated, single-focus learning episodes that are not well situated in an overall framework of intended learning outcomes, and such stand-alone activities are less supportive of conceptual, thorough understanding and growth.

A key aspect of supporting rigorous and comprehensive instruction is to support teachers in recognizing and strengthening alignment of multiple learning experiences to one another and to a broader framework. Thus, for example, when teachers are using critical and creative thinking lessons such as those outlined in Chapter 3, they should be finding ways of situating those learning experiences within a broader understanding of intended outcomes. Written curriculum units that have such integration already built in are, therefore, important models of rigor for teachers and resources for promoting comprehensive learning.

Relevant and Representative

Curriculum is more likely to provide the context for effective learning when students can see the relevance of the learning experience to their own lives. When students feel disconnected from the material and cannot see why it matters to them, they are less likely to be motivated for successful engagement. This issue may be exacerbated for students who come from backgrounds often underserved by advanced academic programs—the very students who are the focus of the Young Scholars Model.

Critical motivators for student learning include giving students choices and allowing them to pursue learning that connects to personal interests. When students are engaged in learning that is meaningful, relevant, and challenging, they are more likely to continue the learning process both in and out of school. For example, one young scholar wrote in her journal:

> I was fishing with my dad in the river and I caught a large fish that looked different from any fish I had ever seen before. When I asked my dad what it was, he explained that it was a snakehead and they were an invasive species. I wanted to learn more so we took a picture of the fish and this is how my research began. . . . One of the things that puzzled me was that this fish was an invasive species and I wanted to know more about that . . . where did they come from? Who brought them here?

In addition to student interests, real-world concerns and problems that connect to students' lives provide students the opportunity to practice and refine critical and creative thinking skills. Further, it is important for students to be able to see themselves in their curricular experiences—authors, characters, and historical figures who look like them, as well as topics and issues that matter in their own lives.

Several features help make curriculum and instruction relevant for students from a wide range of backgrounds. First, a curriculum organized around big ideas and concepts offers multiple entry points. Whatever a student's background, that student has had some experience with *courage, justice, change*, or *systems*. Curriculum that invites students to bring their own experiences of the concepts into the discussion provides greater support for building relevance, and it promotes opportunities for students to understand multiple perspectives. Thus, students are not limited by their background knowledge but rather honored and respected for the individual contributions they can bring.

Second, choices in curriculum should include diverse perspectives and backgrounds in the authors, characters, individuals, and groups reflected in the texts and resources students will encounter. Recent research has highlighted the degree to which individuals from traditionally underserved populations also have limited representation in the curriculum (Harris & Reynolds, 2014; Sano, 2009). Yet it is important for students to see others like themselves in the leaders, thinkers, and creators they study, as well as in the characters and experiences they are encouraged to understand. Thus, across all curricular areas, educators must give attention to diverse, multicultural representation in the resources used. When students are given the opportunity to study diverse leaders who have changed the world for the better, they are able to recognize that the traits and characteristics these people possess cross all lines of color, class, and culture.

Third, curriculum should address real-world problems that matter to students and to their communities. It is important for students to grapple with the major issues that affect the increasingly global society in which we live, but also to understand the ways in which global issues are relevant at a local level—as well as why local issues matter in and of themselves. By focusing on concerns, news items, and important events that address global issues (i.e., economic survival, political decision making, climate change, and human rights) and examining the varied perspectives within their own environment, students learn to think critically about multiple views on issues and seek solutions that are in alignment with a more inclusive, pluralistic view of society. These types of focus areas for curriculum also lend themselves well to authentic assessment opportunities, including experiences that encourage students to share their work with audiences beyond the classroom.

Finally, a curriculum with strong driving questions as a foundation supports motivation. It is important to provide students with opportunities to connect with the content and to have multiple entry points, but it is also important for them to feel that their work is directed toward some goal or answer to a question that matters. Driving questions may be framed within curricular resources, may connect to overarching concepts such as change or systems, or may emerge as students engage with curriculum and determine the nature of the problem they are trying to solve or an issue they are researching. For example, teachers working with students on understanding primary sources from a given historical period may frame the discussion with an overarching question linking to the present (e.g., How does discovery of the past through historical evidence revise our thinking about people, issues, and events?).

Engaging

Along with a focus on rigor and relevance, curriculum should also be planned to support active student engagement. Instructional activities that incorporate student choice, present material in a variety of formats, and encourage student questioning and discussion help to make students co-owners of the learning process and promote their investment and engagement.

Problem-based learning experiences and project-based approaches are particularly useful formats for encouraging student choice and engagement. When teachers and students examine real-world problems and work together to plan and collaborate in understanding and addressing key questions, they bring life, meaning, and purpose to the school experience. Some curriculum is specifically designed around real-world, ill-structured problems that encourage students in the complexity of defining a problem and determining steps for responding to it. Well-designed problem-based materials respond to the developmental level of the student in terms of establishing an issue of interest and provide an important pathway to deeper understanding of the content. Problem-centered themes identified and chosen by students also provide opportunities for students to think critically and make meaningful connections as they explore knowledge in an approach to learning that builds multiple levels of understanding. For example, a whole-class nonfiction project with a unifying theme allows students to search for information on topics of their own choosing, make connections to personal experience, and learn from each other through the sharing and exchange of information as they explore and discover the connections to the overall theme.

Voices From the Field

One of my students wrote,

Several years ago, when I was coming home from Maryland after a long trip, we passed by Calvert Cliffs Nuclear Power Plant. As a curious boy, I begged my parents to stop by the nuclear power plant to see what it would be like. There were many fascinating exhibits there and I was beginning to grow an interest in the subject. I went to the library to check some books out, but at my age, I could not understand a thing. I put the subject in the back of my head and only referred to it if I found anything else that was associated with the topic.

Then this research project came up and I started to do a more extensive search on the subject that I left years ago.

Another student became interested in wetlands after I mentioned a wetlands park that was within easy driving distance of his home. He wrote in his journal,

> I ran to the library and asked the librarian where the books on the wetlands were. I found them and took them back to the table and started to take notes. . . . One of the things that puzzled me was that wetlands are polluted by water pollution. . . . I decided to ask my grandma to take me to the wetlands park so I can learn more about this problem.

Although he initially was unable to make a connection between his topic and a personal experience, the research process generated experiences that would eventually make that connection for him.

Choice and ownership provided intrinsic motivation as each student searched for information on a topic that they truly cared about. The concepts of perception, respect, survival, and responsibility became familiar to them and provided a language that they could use as they connected new information to the generalizations that they had developed during class discussions.

Another learner wrote in her journal, "At first I thought that the rainforests were dangerous places and that the animals in the rainforest eat people. But they don't, so see that was just my perception. I learned that animals eat plants and other animals in the rainforest." She also became fascinated with pictures of rainforest people that she found in old *National Geographic* magazines at the library. She wrote in her journal, "I also thought that there were not any people in the rainforest. But I learned there are tribes of people and their kids don't have to go to school, now I want to find out why." The pictures were the hook, and whereas most children would have focused on the plants and animals, this student focused on the children of the rainforest. Another student also reflected on the concept of perception, but on a more complex level. In his journal, he wrote, "I always thought that nuclear power was somewhat useful but very dangerous. . . . through research my perception has significantly changed. . . . I realize that there is hope for it in the future."

Each student had the opportunity to search for information and reflect on new knowledge in ways that were appropriate for them. I soon discovered that I had several students from low socioeconomic and culturally diverse backgrounds who were able to think more abstractly and with greater complexity than I had initially thought.

—Young Scholars teacher, describing a whole-class nonfiction project on environmental concerns

Open-ended, flexible assignments that encourage student choice while addressing important learning outcomes provide the space to enhance student strengths and promote creativity. Students learn and apply tools of inquiry and habits of mind relevant to the discipline under study while exploring content that is of interest to them. Rather than limiting skill development to brief, prescribed activities, complex projects that incorporate ongoing, performance-based assessments support students in growing their areas of strength and allow teachers to recognize and nurture those strengths. Such projects become a context for assessing a student's ability to apply, transfer, transform, and extend their learning, as they ultimately become producers of new insights in their chosen field of endeavor. Providing choice and ownership in the application of their knowledge and skills increases motivation to learn and inspires students to create products that are a true representation of what they understand and are able to do.

Curriculum also supports student engagement through resources that draw on a range of formats and stimuli. Today's technology supports access to a wealth of visual and audio material that brings faraway places and a wide range of voices into the classroom. Students can take an electronic field trip to numerous places to gain firsthand information on a topic. They can also contact experts in the field through email and video calls and/or participate in web conferences to find answers to their questions and explore topics of interest. Further, such approaches help broaden background knowledge, raise awareness of future possibilities, and support language learning. At the same time, it is also critical for students to engage with concrete materials whenever possible, not just see them in a book or on a screen. Manipulatives in mathematics, tactile materials for exploration and experimentation in science, STEM projects, and a range of other resources are important for enhancing learning and helping students to link classroom learning to the outside world.

In a project-based learning approach, students actively explore and investigate open-ended, meaningful questions that will engage them in an active approach to learning. Topics might range from "Why should we protect wetlands?" to "How can we replicate the work of historians to learn about and share stories about our community?" The possibilities are endless, and the process of selecting a question to investigate can be as engaging as the project itself. Once a topic is selected, students begin learning about the topic in a collaborative setting that supports active and group learning.

Engagement also results from efforts to build connections for students. For example, studying biographies of leaders and innovators in a given discipline, particularly when those biographies discuss the origins of an area of interest in the individual's childhood, can be a useful way to connect students to content (Robinson et al., 2018). In another approach to encouraging engagement, the mathematics units developed under Project M^2 include opportunities for students to communicate with animal characters who help to frame the content under study. Thus, sometimes the questions and tasks come from the pen pal frogs, birds, or meerkats instead of from the teacher; this helps to build motivation and connection in young learners (Gavin et al., 2013).

Finally, engagement is promoted by an active learning environment that encourages curiosity and an exchange of information and ideas. Curriculum framed by driving questions and shaped by ongoing discourse in the classroom allows students to become active partners in the learning process. It also invites varied perspectives, experiences, and stories. A thoughtful selection of curricular resources and instructional strategies will help students make personal connections to the content and increase their understanding of how it is relevant to their current and future lives.

Voices From the Field

As a gifted resource teacher in a high-poverty school, one of my tasks was to organize screening committee meetings including classroom teachers, administrators, counselors, and myself where we would discuss students who need differentiated services. Sometimes I would have teachers who struggled to name any evidence of critical and creative thinking demonstrated by the student under review. When this occurred, my first question was always, "Was the student provided opportunities to develop and demonstrate that type of thinking in the classroom?" In my experience, the answer to this question is crucial to understanding whether those talent development experiences have been provided. After all, how can you spot talent if you don't offer opportunities for students to demonstrate talent? This begins with access to high-quality curricula.

Yet simply implementing high-quality curricula to "check a box" can also fall far short of the goal of talent development. I attribute this to the perspective through which curricula are viewed, either as an objective entity devoid of context or as a subjective entity experienced through interaction with teachers and students. From the first perspective, we may read through the complete teacher's manual, student texts, and any associated materials and think, "This is brilliant! Students will be engaged in tasks that promote higher level thinking if I simply follow all of the instructions." This perspective requires no extra thought from the teacher, who merely becomes the implementer of curriculum, and can lead to statements such as, "But when we did a *Jacob's Ladder* lesson, they didn't do anything to wow me with their thinking."

The second perspective—looking at curricula as subjective entities experienced through interaction—recenters the teacher from consumer or implementer to critical thinker, asking themselves questions such as, "How might I make this accessible to all of my students?" or "How might this curricula provide 'mirrors, windows, and doors' through which my students can explore, construct, and negotiate their identities?" These teachers understand that the cultural and linguistic resources of students in their individual classrooms must be considered and leveraged during implementation and that no curriculum is culturally neutral.

When I hear from teachers implementing high-quality curricula from the latter perspective, they remark on how they are constantly being "wowed" by their students and stretching their own thinking around what students of a certain age are capable of thinking. And I think, in a nutshell, that's what talent development is—not students proving to their teachers that they are capable, but rather teachers reimagining what and how capability might be demonstrated in students.

—Holly Glaser, Young Scholars teacher

Support for Advanced-Level Learners and Learning

Effective curriculum planning is about developing overarching goals for learning over a span of time, considering needed modifications of those goals for varied populations of learners, including advanced learners, and selecting materials that will support progress toward those goals. High-quality implementation of the Young Scholars Model relies in part on the use of existing curriculum materials that have been written with an advanced learner population in mind, or that emphasize the features that are most critical for such a population. Recommendations for curriculum for advanced learners reflect the criteria described previously for high-quality curriculum in general and also emphasize several features that promote challenge and engagement for these learners (Hockett, 2009; VanTassel-Baska & Little, 2017).

Figure 9
Sample Resources Developed With Advanced
Learner Populations as a Key Focus

> ⮞ Project M^2 (http://projectm2.org) and Project M^3 (http://projectm3.org)
> ⮞ Project A^3 (program feature available at https://k12.kendallhunt.com/content/30389/view-demo)
> ⮞ William & Mary mathematics materials (https://education.wm.edu/centers/cfge/curriculum/mathematics/materials/index.php)
> ⮞ William & Mary language arts materials (https://education.wm.edu/centers/cfge/curriculum/languagearts/materials/index.php)
> ⮞ William & Mary social studies materials (https://education.wm.edu/centers/cfge/curriculum/socialstudies/materials/index.php)
> ⮞ William & Mary Navigators (https://education.wm.edu/centers/cfge/curriculum/languagearts/materials/navigators/index.php)
> ⮞ Project Clarion and William & Mary science materials (https://education.wm.edu/centers/cfge/curriculum/science/materials/index.php)
> ⮞ Jacob's Ladder Reading Comprehension Program (https://www.prufrock.com/jacobsladder.aspx)
> ⮞ Jacob's Ladder Reading Comprehension Program: Nonfiction (https://www.prufrock.com/jacobsladder.aspx#Nonfiction)
> ⮞ Affective Jacob's Ladder Reading Comprehension Program (https://www.prufrock.com/jacobsladder.aspx#Affective)
> ⮞ Advanced units from Vanderbilt University (https://www.prufrock.com/vanderbilt-units.aspx)
> ⮞ CLEAR model units from the University of Virginia (https://www.prufrock.com/University-of-Virginia-C1252.aspx)
> ⮞ Blueprints for Biography (https://ualr.edu/gifted/curriculum/blueprints)

There are a number of published curricular resources that are useful in developing a plan for implementation of the Young Scholars Model. In many cases, these resources were developed as part of research initiatives focused specifically on the populations of learners who would be young scholars—students of strong academic potential in groups typically underserved by gifted and talented programs. The Jacob K. Javits Gifted and Talented Students Education Program, a grant program under the U.S. Department of Education, has funded a variety of these projects resulting in resources. See Figure 9 for examples of some of the resources developed under Javits funding and related initiatives.

Figure 10
Additional Sample Resources

- Engineering is Elementary (https://www.eie.org/stem-curricula/engineering-grades-prek-8/engineering-is-elementary)
- JASON Learning (https://jason.org)
- The DBQ Project (https://www.dbqproject.com)
- Engaging With History in the Classroom series (https://www.prufrock.com/Search.aspx?k=engaging+with+history+in+the+classroom)
- Library of Congress primary source resources (https://www.loc.gov/programs/teachers/getting-started-with-primary-sources)
- National Geographic education resources (https://www.nationalgeographic.org/education)

Other curricular resources that are not specifically designed for advanced learners but that nevertheless reflect key features of curriculum for this population are also useful for building a Young Scholars plan. Several organizations have published high-quality materials that have been used in advanced learning programs, including Young Scholars programs, to challenge and engage these learners. See Figure 10 for examples.

In this section, we briefly outline some of the key features that make these types of resources and the instructional approaches they incorporate appropriate for working with advanced learners, and why they are valuable in the context of implementing the Young Scholars Model.

Advanced Content

Engagement with advanced content is a critical component of services for learners who show advanced academic potential. Advanced content may appear in a variety of ways in curricular materials. There may be goals and objectives that are usually not addressed until a more advanced grade level. The reading materials may have a higher level or increased complexity of ideas and language. The materials may also provide advancement through the pace of learning, with less repetition and practice with skills and more combination of ideas and demands into complex tasks.

For some young scholars, the advanced content emphasis of some curricular materials must be paired with scaffolding and support to ensure the background knowledge necessary for engaging with the advanced content. For example, there may be a need for preteaching of vocabulary before young scholars engage with advanced reading materials; this support is a recognition that students are ready for the *ideas* presented but may be unfamiliar with the specific *terms* employed. Other language-learning resources may be important supports for young scholars who are English language learners as they engage with advanced materials.

Sometimes teachers express concerns that engaging learners with the depth of advanced curricular materials will have a negative effect on student performance on standardized tests. Yet evidence from multiple research studies has demonstrated that students tend to show similar or better performance on standardized tests following use of advanced materials compared to similar students not using those materials, as well as show higher performance on other measures of understanding and growth (e.g., Bracken et al., 2007; Gavin et al., 2013; Kim et al., 2012).

Conceptual Focus

A focus on big ideas and interdisciplinary concepts is a useful way of engaging advanced learners with deep thinking and challenging learning. As noted previously, conceptual organization of the curriculum also provides broader entry points for learners. The approach invites learners to come from a place of their own experience of the big ideas and then to build connections to the specific content together.

Several resources designed for advanced-level learning that take a conceptual approach are available for multiple grade levels and content areas. The Integrated Curriculum Model (VanTassel-Baska, 1986, 2017) emphasizes the value of concept-focused curriculum for advanced learners and has been the basis for curriculum in multiple content areas from teams at William & Mary and Vanderbilt University. In some of these resources, students pursue in-depth study of literature or a historical period through the lens of a particular concept, such as *change, perspective*, or *justice*. Thorough analysis of the concept itself, connected with multiple applications of key understandings and generalizations about the concept within content-area resources, deepens student understanding of the central idea and of the discipline under study.

Voices From the Field

The content was enriched with interdisciplinary concepts that related to an overriding theme—the environment. Perception, respect, survival, and responsibility were key concepts woven throughout the curriculum in order to deepen the class's understanding of the Earth and the complexity of environmental issues. Perception was important because I wanted my students to understand how each person sees the world through a unique lens that is colored by prior knowledge and experience. Respect for differences helped us value the uniqueness of each class member and reinforced a stronger sense of community—a community that became committed to protecting and preserving our common home, the Earth. The survival theme permeated all of the disciplines as we learned about the internal and external forces that impact survival on many different levels for individuals, animals, cultures, and nations. Finally, knowledge and awareness led to responsibility for doing what is right for the right reasons. Through reading, reflection, and class discussions, students searched for increased knowledge that could translate into meaningful applications for their lives.

—Young Scholars teacher

Depth and Complexity

Discussions of appropriate curriculum and instruction for advanced learners frequently center around increased depth and complexity compared to the standard curriculum. These terms, which rarely appear singly instead of in combination in discussion of curriculum, reflect several key features of curriculum, including the following:

- focus on big ideas,
- emphasis on looking for patterns and connections,
- multiple perspectives,
- multiple variables,
- attention to rules and trends,
- language and practices of the discipline under study,
- exploring unanswered questions,
- pursuit and presentation of detail, and
- connections across disciplines.

These features appear in most recommendations about curriculum and instruction for advanced learners, and, indeed, in broader recommendations for high-quality curriculum (Kaplan, 2013; VanTassel-Baska & Stambaugh, 2006).

Critical and Creative Thinking Emphasis

Strong infusion of critical and creative thinking skills is an important context for using curriculum as a talent identifier as well as using it to support overall talent development. In many Young Scholars schools, as outlined in Chapter 3, resource teachers partner with classroom teachers to implement model lessons that incorporate specific strategies for critical and creative thinking. These lessons are implemented with all learners to invite students to demonstrate their academic potential. Ongoing use helps to equip learners with strategies they can use to engage with new content throughout schooling and, indeed, in everyday life.

Many resources designed for advanced learners include specific emphasis on applying models for critical and creative thinking. For example, much of the curriculum work built on the Integrated Curriculum Model incorporates a focus on critical thinking as defined by Richard Paul and his collaborators (Paul, 1993; Paul & Elder, 2012). The Creative Problem Solving process (Isaksen et al., 2011) is another approach frequently used to engage students in thinking about complex problem solving. Other resources employ specific models for research, for divergent thinking, and for wrestling with issues and decisions, extending and deepening the kinds of applications of these strategies noted in Chapter 3.

Regular Practice of Teaching Models and Metacognition

High-quality curriculum that is built around solid teaching models promotes engagement with advanced-level learning by helping students become well practiced in using a set of steps or questions to approach new and challenging content. Several of the critical and creative thinking models that frame many of these curricular examples provide this kind of support, because in teaching and practicing the steps and elements of these models, teachers support students in understanding how and why they work. In another example, the mathematics units from Project M^2 and Project M^3 place a strong emphasis on teaching and practicing specific discourse moves during mathematics discussions (Chapin et al., 2003; Gavin et al., 2007, 2013). The extensive practice with the "talk moves" builds students' comfort with them, making it easier for students to engage in discussion about new and challenging mathematics content because they have a well-practiced structure for conversation.

Socratic seminars, similarly, also represent an approach that promotes deeper conversation with challenging content over time because students engage with the practice repeatedly. This approach involves students in deep discussions around selected texts, with emphasis on building connections to other texts and experiences, practicing speaking and listening skills, and using evidence to respond to questions. Students take the lead in developing questions and facilitating discussion in a Socratic seminar, and that student-led emphasis increases over time as students gain more experience with the approach.

With all of these approaches, an added layer of both challenge and support is encouraging students' metacognition as they work with the models and strategies. When teachers guide students to plan, monitor, and evaluate their own engagement with discussion or problem solving or thinking about an issue, they support students' developing ability to know when and how they might use these strategies effectively.

Appropriate Assessment Approaches

The assessment approaches incorporated into curriculum for advanced learners should reflect attention to the issue that these learners are often capable of working well above grade-level standards, and thus regular grade-level assessments may not provide sufficient scope for students to show what they can do. When students always "top out" or score at the highest possible levels on assessments, the assessments do not have enough of a ceiling to provide useful information about these students' progress and needs. Further, learners begin any new unit at different stages of readiness, and it is important for teachers to have a strong sense at the beginning of the unit of what students already know—both to provide support and scaffolding for students who need that support to access the material, and to ensure that the material is not repetitive or too simple for students who are already ahead. Appropriate differentiation cannot happen without a preassessment. Thus, it is important for assessment approaches to include preassessment, ongoing assessment, and postassessments; to be varied in their form; and to provide a wide range of possible performance levels.

Assessment processes and considerations should also include attention to authentic questions and authentic products for authentic audiences. Authentic questions are those that do not have simple or straightforward answers, but that represent new learning that participating students are motivated to explore. The audience for assessments in school is often just the teacher, or the teacher and other students in the classroom, but an authentic audience adds to the motivation and possibility for feedback for learners.

Grouping Strategies

One key organizational component of the Young Scholars Model that is linked to curriculum as well as other aspects is the importance of grouping. Deliberate grouping of young scholars is essential to ensure that they have opportunities to work with other students like themselves and to support each other in approaching new academic challenges.

Such grouping may be accomplished in multiple ways in connection with the curriculum and the overall implementation of the model. First, schools implementing Young Scholars at the elementary and middle level should consider a cluster grouping approach (Gentry & Fugate, 2013), putting several young scholars together in the same classes with teachers who have participated in professional learning around supporting these learners' needs. This approach facilitates in-class instructional grouping and allows teachers to use a more targeted approach to differentiation. Consistent flexible grouping should be part of the approach in any classroom, with recognition that students show different learning patterns with different new skills and content. Further, schools may use additional grouping approaches to engage young scholars, including providing specific interventions for small groups as needed.

Focus on Affective and Academic Needs

Most of the discussion in this chapter has focused on addressing the academic needs of students who are young scholars, but it is also important to note their affective needs and the relevance of curriculum and instruction for responding to those needs. As students engage with big ideas and advanced materials, teachers also provide support for students' emotional response to texts, their social interactions with one another, and their overall affective development. Such efforts may be supported by curricular resources, such as the Jacob's Ladder Reading Comprehension Program materials for affective development (e.g., VanTassel-Baska & Stambaugh, 2020), which engage students in discussion around key areas of social and emotional growth. Further, school teams may provide specific opportunities for young scholars to work together and work with teachers and counselors to develop self-efficacy, to talk about their approach to solving problems in the face of challenge, and to develop and practice other social and emotional skills (Durlak et al., 2011).

Connections to District-Level Collaborations and Professional Learning

Effective implementation of the Young Scholars Model requires articulating the key emphases of curriculum to be employed with young scholars, how such curriculum is organized across grades and subjects, and how it aligns with other curriculum initiatives. A central theme of this text is that Young Scholars is not an "add-on" to other initiatives, but rather that it should be integrated with other goals and initiatives going on in the school at the same time. Thus, planning efforts related to Young Scholars should incorporate attention to the broader goals and initiatives of the school and district, and planning efforts linked to those broader goals and initiatives should include consideration of Young Scholars.

For example, one school system increasingly felt that there was a need for broader access to advanced academic curriculum for all students. The curriculum used in advanced academics was aligned to broader district goals to increase rigor and provide more opportunities for student-centered instruction, such as concept-based and inquiry-based instruction. District leaders recognized that increasing the use of gifted education pedagogy and recording student responses to a high-level curriculum could provide important evidence of advanced potential in students who may not score well on standardized tests. They also realized that this was an action that needed to be used more consistently across the district. Consequently, they increased gifted resource teacher staffing at Title I elementary schools. They also increased professional learning opportunities for all teachers that centered on using advanced curriculum for talent seeking. Further planning efforts resulted in a decision that every elementary teacher would use at least one advanced curriculum resource with all learners at least once each year.

Curriculum planning for Young Scholars requires first having a "seat at the table" during discussions of curriculum planning in general. School and district leaders who are spearheading Young Scholars implementation must work on building relationships with many other leaders in the district, including those who have leadership responsibilities for curriculum in general and in specific content areas. Such relationships can help to facilitate active consideration of advanced and high-potential learners in discussions around scope and sequence planning, pacing guides, and curriculum adoption. Further, these relationships promote attention to the needs of young scholars in planning for professional learning and allocation of resources. The use of high-quality curriculum as a centerpiece of Young Scholars intersects directly with the professional learning demands of implementing the model. The emphasis on advanced learning opportunities to seek unidentified talent also has the potential to support increases in access to rigor for all students.

In another school district example, one district's science office wanted to add more rigor for all students in middle school. They also wanted to promote a common language around curriculum and lesson development. Leaders in the science office and the gifted services office collaborated and decided to incorporate a wider focus on problem-based learning, including materials that incorporated a conceptual focus, emphasis on thinking like a scientist, and other key aspects of challenge and engagement. The team developed a professional learning plan with several key components:

- An initial workshop with an outside expert was offered to support sixth-, seventh-, and eighth-grade teachers in developing a common understanding of problem-based learning process.
- Curricular units were purchased for each teacher who attended, with the expectation that they would implement the unit. Differentiated support was given to teachers in a variety of ways, such as planning, implementing in a coteaching structure, and reflection on implementation with the science specialist and/or resource teacher for the gifted.
- There were observation days, as part of countywide professional learning opportunities, during which teachers could observe other teachers implementing the unit.
- After participating in the training and implementing a unit and/or lessons, grade-level teams were offered planning days during which they looked for additional opportunities to implement another problem-based learning unit. As a team, they began the process of writing a scenario and were guided in this practice by the science specialist.
- The team implemented the scenario as a pilot with students and then revised based on experiences of teachers and students.
- Follow-up training was offered to new science teachers each year, as well as countywide sessions offering ongoing support with the problem-based learning process.

Professional learning opportunities for teachers specifically linked to the curriculum materials are essential to effective implementation of the model. Chapter 5 provides more extensive discussion about professional learning as an ongoing emphasis of the Young Scholars Model, but it is worth emphasizing here that direct experience with the curriculum materials in a professional learning environment is a critical foundation, facilitated by support from leadership to ensure teachers have opportunities to access such learning and have resources in their hands. Further, sustained professional learning activities, including such approaches as coaching support and professional learning communities, might incorporate a focus on curricular materials and the questions that arise during their use.

Evaluating and Strengthening Curriculum Implementation to Support Young Scholars

Use of high-quality, challenging curriculum is a central component of the model, and a school's Young Scholars team should establish plans for ongoing evaluation and continuous improvement around efforts to implement such curriculum effectively with learners. This includes attention to ensuring access to the curriculum, enhancing teacher self-efficacy in implementing the curriculum, and strengthening schoolwide efforts to recognize and respond to talent development emerging through curricular experiences. It also includes a focus on fidelity of implementation for curriculum and strong integration between individual units and a larger curriculum framework. Figure 11 provides a sample checklist for a school team to use in reviewing this aspect of the Young Scholars Model.

Part of the effort to implement Young Scholars relies on consistent messaging around the importance of maintaining challenge and rigor in the curriculum that these students experience. This issue is a consideration for leaders of a Young Scholars initiative both at the larger organizational level, with emphasis on curriculum selection, and at the level of providing support for teachers in classrooms in terms of the quality of curriculum implementation.

Often, particularly with populations that tend to be underrepresented in advanced learning programs, there is a strong focus on closing achievement gaps, addressing areas of weakness/low performance, and building basic skills. Although these are certainly worthwhile emphases, they contribute to the lack of rigor and limited challenge that high-potential learners from these populations often experience, and they reduce the effect of the strength-based focus that is a key aspect of talent development. Indeed, one of the defining characteristics of advanced learners is that they need advanced materials earlier than their age peers and are likely to progress through content and skills more quickly than their peers. The "seat at the table" for leaders focused on Young Scholars allows ongoing discussion of the need for access to advanced learning and a focus on strengths, as well as to

Figure 11
Sample Implementation Checklist: High-Quality Curriculum and Instruction

High-Quality Curriculum and Instruction	Level of Implementation			
	Low			High
A curriculum framework that outlines materials, resources, and curricula that are research-based and designed for advanced learners in the four core subjects of mathematics, language arts, social studies, and science guides instruction at all grade levels.				
Teachers use flexible instructional groupings at all grade levels and are committed to providing a growth mindset culture with high-end curriculum and instruction.				
Teachers infuse gifted education pedagogy into teaching practice for all students.				
Students are encouraged to become self-directed learners through independent study projects, problem-based learning, and project-based learning.				
Digital learning is embedded in instruction, and technology is integrated in both process and product of curricular experiences.				
Teachers codevelop a curriculum framework that outlines materials, resources, and curricula that may be used at each grade level to challenge and engage students who are ready for advanced levels of learning.				

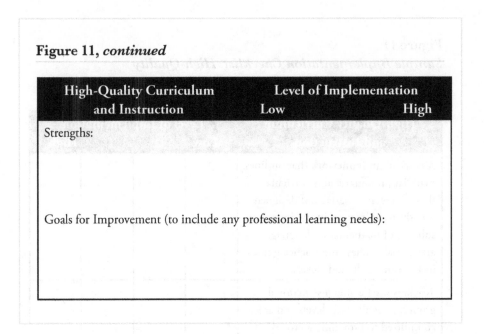

Figure 11, *continued*

High-Quality Curriculum and Instruction	Level of Implementation	
	Low	High
Strengths:		
Goals for Improvement (to include any professional learning needs):		

make these considerations a priority in planning for curriculum and professional learning.

Entry Points and Growth Edges
for the Role of Curriculum

A strong Young Scholars Model may take shape from a grassroots effort, but the true power of the model depends on systemic alignment and coherence. Figure 12 shows some sample indicators that may reveal entry points and growth edges around the role of curriculum as an important component to Young Scholars Model implementation.

Figure 12
*Indicators of Entry Points and Growth Edges
for Curriculum Implementation*

Beginning Implementation	Developing Implementation	Deep Implementation and Monitoring for Improvement Areas
☙ Instructional opportunities are mostly episodic (e.g., focused on strategies). ☙ Instructional opportunities are connected to larger learning goals, but connections may be loosely coupled.	☙ Strategies are embedded within a larger curriculum experience framework. ☙ Some but not all essential elements of a strong curriculum framework (e.g., assessment for growth, conceptual focus, responsive differentiation practices, considerations of interdisciplinary content standards) are in place. ☙ Teachers use curriculum with fidelity.	☙ Curriculum is planned with outcomes for access to rigor and strategies as a means to meet unit goals. ☙ Most or all essential elements of a strong written curriculum framework are in place. ☙ Teachers use curriculum with fidelity and are able to articulate how aspects of the curriculum support deeper learning and student growth. ☙ Units are developed with consideration of culturally responsive principles (e.g., developing student identity and agency). ☙ Structures for documenting student interests and growth areas are embedded and systemic.

Chapter 5

Professional Learning

> When a flower does not bloom, you fix the environment in which it grows, not the flower.
>
> —Alexander den Heijer

Professional learning and growth are a centerpiece of effective implementation of the Young Scholars Model. The model rests on a schoolwide effort to support talent seeking and talent development, and such an effort relies on the engagement of all educators in the learning context. District and school leaders seeking to implement the Young Scholars Model must include specific commitments to support professional learning as a consistent and ongoing part of that effort, including promoting new professional learning and developing professional networks and collaborative teams to achieve program goals. Further, emphasis on Young Scholars as a professional learning initiative should be integrated with other goals for professional growth in a building and in a district.

We believe . . .

- Effective professional learning initiatives are ongoing, valued, and supported through allocation of collaborative learning time, coaching in context, and opportunities for teachers at multiple entry levels to access learning appropriate to their needs.
- A central part of professional learning is engaging with educators' attitudes and mindsets, including the development of inclusive perspectives on talent and talent development as well as cultural responsiveness.
- Professional learning activities that emphasize culturally responsive teaching and strategies for nurturing high potential in all populations help educators to develop a deeper understanding of the need to identify and support academic strengths as they are manifested within the context of each student's current life experiences.
- Effective efforts to support professional learning include opportunities for active engagement, choices for participants, and ongoing support structures that promote application of learning in practice with individual and collaborative reflection.
- In addition to the specific content of the initiative, comprehensive professional learning goals include a focus on building networks of collegial relationships in the school and district contexts for the purposes of organizational learning and continuous improvement.

In this chapter . . .

- We discuss why professional learning is central to effective Young Scholars implementation.
- We outline key content of professional learning for supporting the Young Scholars Model.
- We provide suggested formats and outlines for professional learning for the Young Scholars Model.
- We suggest benchmarks for assessing quality and influence of professional learning initiatives.

The emphasis on ongoing professional learning connects to all four parts of the Young Scholars Model, with heaviest focus on committed professionals and essential elements:

Committed Professionals. The commitment of school professionals to the model is critical to implementation at every stage, from recognizing a need and initiating the model, to ensuring attention to continuous improvement.

Find and Identify. Recognizing potential and identifying talent rely on the efforts of school professionals. Other stakeholders also play a role, but professionals within the school are central to providing opportunities for students to demonstrate potential and supporting access to advanced learning opportunities. Thus, ongoing professional learning is necessary to ensure that teachers and other professionals have the tools that they need to find and identify students.

Nurture, Guide, and Support. Professional learning, from an organizational standpoint, is the vehicle through which leaders can support and facilitate instructional practices that challenge and nurture students' talent development.

Essential Elements. An organized and strategic plan with ongoing support for professional learning is a critical element of effective implementation of the Young Scholars Model. Professional learning opportunities related to Young Scholars can occur in a variety of contexts, including scheduled workshops, ongoing discussions, and opportunities to observe teaching practices with young scholars.

Why Professional Learning Matters for Young Scholars Implementation

Teachers, counselors, classroom assistants, administrators, and other school personnel who work daily with students have frequent opportunities to notice the evidence of advanced potential—the questions students ask, the ways that they engage with new learning, and the connections that they build as they deepen their understanding. It is critical, however, for educators to have a strong understanding of the kinds of behaviors to look for as they think about how high potential can be demonstrated.

Research over several decades has demonstrated that teachers who have had limited training in gifted education tend to have narrow views of high potential that do not reflect contemporary understanding of the behaviors that might indicate high potential in diverse populations of learners (Harradine et al., 2014; Miller, 2009; Moon & Brighton, 2008; Speirs Neumeister et al., 2007; Swanson, 2006). That "limited training" tends to be the rule and not the exception for general education teachers because few teacher preparation programs require coursework in gifted education, and inservice professional learning on gifted education topics also tends to be limited. Narrow understanding of gifted potential connects to narrowed expectations in how teachers think about the learners with whom they work, which then also translates to students' own self-perceptions. The report of the Committee on Minority Representation in Special Education (Donovan & Cross, 2002) underscored the important role that teachers play by emphasizing how the expectations that teachers have for children from diverse backgrounds can greatly impact the expectations that these children have for themselves.

Nevertheless, other studies have demonstrated that high-quality professional learning activities can support and develop teacher perspectives on talent development, broadening their perspective on high potential and encouraging recognition of advanced behaviors in diverse populations (Bangel et al., 2010; Harradine et al., 2014). Teachers also benefit from professional learning activities that are focused on curricular materials and instructional strategies for supporting advanced learning, with increases over time in their implementation of differentiation to respond to advanced learners and their efforts to integrate critical and creative thinking activities. Further, professional learning activities are more likely to influence lasting change in practice if they are sustained over time and include opportunities for teachers to try out and observe results in their own classrooms (Garet et al., 2001).

At the core of professional learning as a foundation for Young Scholars, it is critical for schools and districts to develop shared perspectives around talent development and the need to seek and develop talent in students from all backgrounds. Part of the professional learning initiative starts with the efforts of a school-based Young Scholars leadership team that meets to develop some statements expressing shared values and understandings around talent development and the importance of a strength-oriented focus. Such statements can then serve as the seeds for professional learning goals for the school.

There are several key perspectives on learning and learners that support the success of a Young Scholars initiative, and it is useful for a team implementing the model to begin conversations about these perspectives early on, to promote buy-in, common language, and schoolwide commitment. Each of the following ideas is an important contributor to the goals of Young Scholars:

- **Culturally responsive teaching** (Gay, 2018) is a foundation for supporting demonstration and development of talent. Educators who approach teaching with respect for and responsiveness to students' backgrounds provide the context for students to engage with learning, bring their own experiences to bear on new questions and connections, and grow their skills and talents.

- Educators should be **talent scouts instead of deficit detectors** (Siegle, 2020). All too often, the work of education focuses on what students cannot yet do or are struggling to do rather than on building around what they can do. With students from underserved populations in particular, there is a strong tendency to lean into a deficit focus, instead of seeking and providing opportunities for students to show their strengths. The latter approach bolsters rather than degrades students' sense of efficacy and scholarly identity.

- **Scaffolding and challenge** are complementary emphases, not opposing emphases. Some students are highly capable of engaging with advanced learning activities but may need some scaffolding to access aspects of the experience. For example, if a teacher is implementing a critical and creative thinking strategy such as Fluency, Originality, Flexibility, and Elaboration (FOFE), some students may need the scaffolding of understanding the vocabulary in the title and preceding steps in the lesson and/or may benefit from an example or modeling of each FOFE step.

- **Productive struggle** is a valuable part of learning. It is important for students to be faced with challenging tasks, and part of that challenge is likely to be figuring out the source of the difficulty they are having and how to take next steps (Warshauer, 2015). Sometimes, in keeping with the importance of scaffolding noted previously, teachers may provide support that actually reduces the cognitive demand of a task and thus the opportunity for growth through productive struggle (Jacobs et al., 2014). Thus, it is important to equip students with strategies for approaching a challenging task with perseverance and resilience. Teachers may need opportunities to discuss and clarify not only the importance of scaffolding and support, but also the value of productive struggle.

- **Flexibility** is critical for educators as they strive to recognize students' needs and respond to them in the moment. With true differentiation, teachers use preassessments and ongoing assessments to drive appropriately challenging instruction. Often, students may learn new material more quickly or easily than expected. When this happens, teachers may use flexible instructional grouping to move students to more challenging tasks. Other times, students may run into a roadblock because of an unforeseen gap in their learning or a misconception about the content. In this case, it is important to take a step back and address these issues to support more effective learning and to prepare them for future lessons. As with ongoing assessments and flexibility, teachers will often have to plan appropriate scaffolding and supports for each group. For this reason, it is also important for the teachers to have small-group structures in place to allow for direct instruction with a few while giving the rest of the class opportunities to explore content through independent, respectful tasks.

Starting from these principles, a school-based Young Scholars team might work to develop some core statements that frame how the model will be enacted within the school. Then, one key follow-up to that framing would be considering how these core statements might inform professional learning activities, along with a consideration of questions such as the following:

- ➢ What professional learning opportunities are available to teachers in your district around talent development, differentiation, advanced curricular resources, and excellence gaps in education?
- ➢ Which teachers take advantage of these opportunities (e.g., Do classroom teachers, special education teachers, English language teachers, etc., participate so that they are engaged in talent development efforts?)?
- ➢ Which of these professional learning opportunities can you tap into to show the connection to the mission of Young Scholars?
- ➢ How can you collaborate with other educators so that the Young Scholars vision becomes an integrated part of districtwide and schoolwide initiatives and presentations?
- ➢ What formats for professional learning are available, and do you have opportunities for both formal and job-embedded options to increase support for enacting professional learning around the content?

Key Content of Professional Learning Efforts in Young Scholars Schools

Professional learning around the Young Scholars Model should be aligned with other professional learning goals and emphases within the school and district while also supporting a specific focus on key elements of the model, the core beliefs and perspectives that underlie it, and the specific practices that support it. Content referenced throughout this text would be relevant for professionals developing the implementation of the Young Scholars Model, and our purpose in this chapter is not to provide the full substance of the content, but rather to recommend key areas of emphasis.

The content of professional learning for finding, nurturing, and supporting young scholars might be organized into five large, interrelated categories, with subtopics relevant to each. These categories are briefly outlined in the following sections.

Talent Development and Behaviors Indicating Advanced Potential

Young Scholars is fundamentally about drawing out, nurturing, and developing talents in students from a wide range of backgrounds and experiences. This focus on talent development requires an understanding of what kinds of student behaviors might be indicative of advanced potential in particular domains, how to draw out and encourage those behaviors, and how to support students in developing them to the next level. Further, this focus requires a perspective on education that is strength-based, a mindset that talent potential exists across all populations and backgrounds, and questioning that probes the influence of cultural differences that may influence teacher awareness of student strengths outside of dominant culture norms.

Given these emphases, one element of professional learning should include exploration of the concept of talent development itself. Educators should have opportunities to examine and discuss how talent may be demonstrated and important ways of nurturing it. Professional learning efforts should also include discussion of the types of behaviors that indicate advanced potential in particular areas of talent, including those behaviors that teachers typically expect but also the ones they may not have considered.

In addition to examining behaviors that are indicators of talent, educators should also have learning opportunities focused on different types of assessment and how results of different assessments should be interpreted to understand student needs and strengths. For example, teachers may not have considered that a test score at the highest percentile levels does not actually give a clear picture of a child's ability, because they may have hit a "ceiling" on the test. Also, teachers may not have a strong understanding of how discrepancies between scores on different types of assessments may indicate an underachievement issue or a disability in one area or another. Teachers may also not have a strong sense of how an off-level assessment may provide useful information for understanding the strengths and needs of students showing advanced potential.

Culturally Responsive Teaching

Successful implementation of the Young Scholars Model requires a perspective on education that acknowledges and respects the different backgrounds that students bring to the classroom and draws upon the funds of knowledge within communities. Culturally responsive teaching is the result of a systematic and concerted effort on the part of a number of researchers to develop and implement a theory of culturally responsive pedagogy that draws upon the child's cultural and language strengths while asking schools and teachers to change practice to capitalize on these strengths (Gay, 2018; Matthews & Castellano, 2014). It seeks greater congruence between the culture of the child and the culture of the school to improve academic achievement.

Although children with advanced potential can be found in every level of society and in every cultural and ethnic group, children from economically disadvantaged backgrounds, children of color, and those who are learning English are not being identified for participation in gifted programs in numbers that are proportionate to their representation in the school-age population (Ford, 2010; Hamilton et al., 2018; Olszewski-Kubilius & Thomson, 2010). Research studies show that students with potential for future success who are being raised in poverty are less likely to be identified for participation in programs that would develop their exceptional talents (Hamilton et al., 2018; Peters et al., 2019). Further, most existing programs focus on the problems these children bring to school rather than on areas of strength that can be nurtured and developed (Plucker & Peters, 2016). Learning about culturally responsive teaching through a series of professional learning opportunities affords teachers the opportunity to examine their own knowledge and backgrounds in relation to the children they teach.

Although opportunities for teachers to engage in self-reflection and personal growth opportunities as they relate to culturally responsive teaching practices are critical, many school systems are also conducting countywide curriculum audits with a focus on cultural responsiveness, equity, and representation that will have a wider impact. Through these audits, administrators and teachers will have many opportunities to make direct correlations between the curriculum audit work, talent development, and the implementation of the Young Scholars Model.

Professional Learning to Support Opportunities for Students in Poverty

Pedagogical practices in classrooms of low-income schools range broadly, but overwhelmingly include a menu of more directive practices, such as giving information, reviewing assignments, or asking lower level questions (Thadani et al., 2010). These practices, often aimed at maintaining control and a test prep focus, make up what has been coined "the pedagogy of poverty" and focus instruction on teacher actions for accountability rather than student actions for learning (Haberman, 2010). Poverty affects students physically, socially, emotionally, and cognitively, with cumulative effects the longer a student is in the environment (Evans, 2004; Jensen, 2019). Research in multiple branches of neuroscience and developmental psychology suggests that childhood poverty affects brain development and can have implications for learning through adulthood (Dike, 2017). Deficits in nutrition, sleep, and exercise affect learning, and conditions such as chronic stress can affect working memory, impulse regulation, visual-spatial skills, language, and cognitive development (Dike, 2017).

Through professional learning about how to support students in poverty with self-regulation and higher level curriculum, teachers will learn multiple benefits that will support talent development. Metacognitive strategies, particularly those for deeper processing, have been shown to provide long-term benefits for K–12 student performance with higher effects for students from low socioeconomic backgrounds compared to their more affluent peers (de Boer et al., 2018). As another example, it is important to shift perceptions that may mistake student attention, compliance, or even entertainment as engagement; instead, professional learning can support focusing on the ways that the pedagogical approaches evoke student curiosity and impel students to engage with and feel intrigued by instruction rather than merely follow directions. All of this will provide an important set of teaching moves that will better support talent development for students from low-income backgrounds (Berger et al., 2016).

Curriculum and Instruction to Support Advanced Learning

A fourth key area of emphasis for professional learning efforts linked to Young Scholars is the focus on curricular resources and instructional approaches that provide the supports that these students need to engage with advanced learning and develop their talents. This broad area includes professional learning linked to specific resources (e.g., workshops on specific curricular materials and resources, such as Project M² and Project M³, Jacob's Ladder Reading Comprehension Program, Project Clarion, Engineering is Elementary, or the DBQ Project), as well as professional learning activities linked to specific instructional emphases (e.g., critical and creative thinking strategies, ways of promoting depth in conceptual understanding, and strategies for building background and vocabulary knowledge as scaffolds to support access to advanced learning).

Workshops on these types of resources and strategies are not sufficient to support deep implementation. Although we know professional learning around high-quality curricular resources will raise engagement and provide teachers with multiple opportunities to observe their students' talents, classroom teachers may not embrace the idea of implementing a new resource they are not familiar with or trust that it will teach the necessary skills or content. The Young Scholars team, particularly any resource teachers on the team, will need to seek collaborative opportunities with grade-level teams or individual teachers to model resources with students while classroom teachers observe the lesson and the demonstrated behaviors of the students. Then a resource teacher and classroom teacher can reflect on the implementation and the work products students developed. This is also a time to build on the professional learning opportunity by discussing next steps with this curricular resource and needed supports.

Such practice efforts and collaborative reflection can happen in multiple learning contexts, but one valuable structure that provides a safe place for teachers to try out new materials and approaches with ongoing support and without risk is within a summer school program. Teachers have shared that it helps to have time to practice and implement high-level curriculum and instruction with young scholars in afterschool or summer school settings. It gives them an opportunity to learn and implement high-powered curriculum and instruction without the additional responsibilities that they have during the school year. Many teachers are amazed at what students are capable of doing when stretched and challenged through the use of curriculum and practices that have been historically reserved for identified gifted learners. Teachers also feel more confident in using the strategies and practices during the school year after they have had the opportunity to practice them successfully during the summer or in an afterschool setting. This is a direct result of the intentional professional learning around resources and ongoing coaching and support during implementation in summer school.

Through professional learning experiences, summer school and afterschool opportunities for students, and the work of collaborative teams, the teachers in Young Scholars schools begin to take a multidimensional look at evidence of potential talent through a review of daily learning activities, performance assessments, and interactions with their students.

Voices From the Field

I was a summer program teacher for 5 years and taught kindergarten, first, or second grade during those summers. Every year was different and rewarding in its own way, but one thought came to me each summer and stayed with me: "This is exactly how we should be teaching math during the school year in our regular classrooms."

We worked each summer in pairs of teachers or with students and/or paraprofessionals to help us. We had a rich curriculum and leaders from [the Young Scholars team] to support and guide us through the lessons. We were given feedback that helped us to reflect and shape lessons.

The most powerful piece, however, was the small class size combined with this challenging curriculum. This setup afforded us the opportunity to teach individually and to meet and challenge each student where they were.

One surprise for me was the carryover of learning and responding to the school year. I realized I was getting solid professional development that would affect my teaching during the year. However, I didn't realize how the young scholars would emerge in our regular classrooms as leaders not only during math instruction but during other subjects as well. Without prompting, these students would say things like, "I agree . . . and here's my thinking . . ." or "I can add on to that. . . ."

This natural progression was so startling and led to classrooms that were much more student-driven and accepting of risk-taking and growth. We all benefited—teachers, young scholars, and other students—from the experience during this time, and this continues now in our schools.

—Lisa Kropp, classroom teacher and Young Scholars summer school teacher

Young Scholars "Nuts and Bolts"

A fifth area for professional learning linked to Young Scholars is very different from yet integrally connected to the other three—engaging educators with the logistics and details of making Young Scholars work in the school. This one might not emerge as a specific workshop topic for teachers, but it is nevertheless critical content that should be integrated with all of the others to help teachers envision, understand, and evaluate how Young Scholars works and how it is integrated with other school initiatives. This emphasis is, by necessity, tailored to the specific context of the school or district in which the model is being implemented, and it includes attention to the procedural as well as the cultural shifts that the model represents within a school and district.

Formats for Professional Learning Activities in Support of the Young Scholars Model

Goals and approaches to professional learning linked to the Young Scholars Model need to be comprehensive, integrated, sustained, and tailored to specific professional needs:

- **Comprehensive.** Comprehensive professional learning activities incorporate consideration of all of the major content components outlined previously, in addition to the logistical elements for making Young Scholars work in the specific school environment. The overall professional learning plan for Young Scholars in a school or district should include specific goals for educator learning, strategies for implementation, and approaches for assessing progress and encouraging self-evaluation of growth. A menu of professional learning opportunities, focused on the elements of the model, motivates staff to select the courses and workshops that meet their professional learning needs and help them develop their own thorough understanding. For example, although some teachers have an endorsement in gifted education, they may need to learn about how to provide scaffolds and supports for young scholars and other students with specific learning needs. Other teachers may be proficient in best practices in specific subject areas but want to learn about infusing higher level thinking strategies into teaching and learning in their classrooms.

- **Integrated.** The leadership team guiding the implementation of Young Scholars makes a concerted effort to demonstrate the alignment of the model with other initiatives and goals of the school and district, and to outline specific ways that the educators in the building can address integrated goals efficiently and effectively. This requires strong communication and collaboration among leaders as they work to ensure alignment and consistent messaging. It also requires the leadership team to recognize and address situations in which conflicting messages or demands emerge, with attention to progress toward the overall goals for growth and student support. Giving staff time to discuss and make connections between the goals of the model and overarching district goals is time well spent and will help alleviate any concerns that this is "just one more initiative."

∾ **Sustained.** Professional learning is not a single event; it is a process that must be sustained and nurtured over time, with a variety of approaches and opportunities for professionals to engage in ongoing conversation as they learn, apply, and reflect on strategies and ways of thinking about talent development.

∾ **Tailored.** Educators in any context vary in their stages of professional growth, readiness for particular topics and approaches, and mindset about the content of their learning. Further, different educators play different roles in implementing Young Scholars, so their learning needs also vary by position and role. Just like their students, educators benefit from learning opportunities that incorporate some differentiation to respond to their needs. Some of this tailoring may occur through menus of professional learning options. This is especially useful for face-to-face learning events, such as summer institutes with a variety of sessions and topics, or virtual learning through a targeted list of webinars. Other tailoring may occur through supportive coaching, group decision making about topics and goals to pursue in small learning groups, and individual choices to pursue more advanced understanding. The professional learning approach should also include an emphasis on active goal setting and progress monitoring from individual educators themselves.

Effective implementation of the Young Scholars Model cannot grow from educator participation in a one-day, one-shot workshop about the model, although such a workshop may form one part of a more comprehensive professional learning plan. Given the complexity of topics and intended outcomes related to the model, as well as what we know about effective practice in professional learning, the learning experiences for educators must extend far beyond offering brief, stand-alone workshops or an afterschool meeting. Commitment to effective development of a Young Scholars school includes a consistent focus on professional learning that takes multiple formats and that includes introductory and more advanced learning opportunities that recognize varied learning needs among educators.

Workshops

Workshops for educators are an important part of (although not the entirety of) a professional learning plan for a school or district implementing Young Scholars. Intensive workshops provide a context for teams of teachers to hear a common message, explore key ideas collaboratively, and engage in modeling some of the classroom-based practices they are seeking to learn (Little & Paul, 2009). When workshops are incorporated as part of a broader professional learning plan, they can provide an important context for introducing content and providing discussion space for teachers to work through their questions. Further, a workshop series might support some of the sustained learning and follow-up that is critical for making change happen in classrooms.

For example, a district or school might commit to a series of workshops to support Young Scholars implementation across the course of a year, to be supplemented by other forms of professional learning. In a smaller school or district context, these workshops might have to be offered as one series, but in a larger district, each workshop could be offered multiple times, giving teachers options to choose from a menu based on their own progress and needs. Workshops might also be offered as summer learning opportunities for educators through some kind of intensive institute. See Figure 13 for sample workshop topics relevant to the Young Scholars Model.

As leaders of the implementation of a Young Scholars Model plan and design workshop offerings, they should draw on not only details of the model itself, but also efforts to assess needs at the building and district level. Leaders can collect feedback formally and informally from educators involved with Young Scholars and consider professional learning needs of different individuals and groups. For example, resource teachers engaged in collaborative support for classroom teachers may have different concerns and questions from the classroom teachers themselves, based on their different perspectives and past professional learning experiences. Further, administrators, counselors, and others involved in school-wide Young Scholars efforts also have professional learning needs related to implementing the model, but these individuals have different responsibilities and thus different learning needs related to implementing it.

Coursework and Online Modules

Some districts may have the capability and structures to support more in-depth, formal coursework relevant for school personnel engaged in Young Scholars work. Such courses may in some cases be offered by universities, potentially in collaboration with school districts, as a way of promoting further professional learning. Courses on gifted and talented education are relevant, as are courses on culturally responsive teaching, leadership for school reform and promoting equity, and other topics that build on the content outlined here. Increased avail-

Figure 13
Sample Workshop Topics

Big Ideas Around Young Scholars	Encouraging and Eliciting Talents
❧ Talent development: What is it, and what does it mean for practice? ❧ Culturally responsive practices ❧ Strengthening relationships with students ❧ Strengthening relationships with families ❧ Promoting and sustaining a growth mindset	❧ What do gifted behaviors from diverse populations look like, and how can we elicit them in the classroom? ❧ Using critical and creative thinking strategies to draw out behaviors and highlight strengths ❧ Using interest surveys to raise the level of engagement of young scholars ❧ Promoting engagement in individualized, project-oriented learning
Tools and Resources for Identifying and Supporting Young Scholars	**Working With Young Scholars**
❧ What do assessments of ability and achievement tell us about learners? ❧ Talent potential in diverse populations ❧ How to use digital portfolios to show growth over time	❧ Curriculum-specific workshops (e.g., Project M² or Project M³, JASON Learning, Jacob's Ladder Reading Comprehension Program) and respectful scaffolding ❧ Concept-focused instruction ❧ Instructional strategies that promote depth and complexity ❧ Problem-based learning ❧ Building background knowledge while supporting advanced learning ❧ Appropriate and respectful scaffolding while offering opportunities for perseverance and resilience

ability of high-quality online coursework can increase opportunities for practicing educators to pursue further learning, again either through existing or developing university-based courses or experiences provided through a school district.

For example, the original Young Scholars leadership team developed an online course on the model that might be replicated in other learning contexts for districts, schools, or individuals seeking a more formalized professional learning approach. Districts might develop a full course or individual modules that engage educators in activities such as these:

- examining case studies of individual young scholars to make recommendations around appropriate services,
- conducting a reflective self-study of current practices to determine specific areas of need in a school,
- reading and discussing perspectives on talent development in diverse populations, and
- developing, practicing, and evaluating learning activities that will elicit demonstration of high-potential behaviors from learners.

Districts may also develop online modules related to some of the specific resources to be used in Young Scholars classrooms and/or in summer and after-school programs. Introductory modules that provide an overview of particular strategies or materials can help to front-load information teachers will need, as well as being a resource they can return to for review as they work more deeply in learning about and implementing strategies.

Professional Learning Communities

As school leadership teams guide the implementation of Young Scholars, they can promote sustained professional engagement through strategies that emphasize that professional learning is about building relationships as much as it is about developing knowledge. Professional learning communities and other strategies that prioritize time for teachers to learn collaboratively help to build and sustain a shared commitment to the goals of Young Scholars. Groups of educators come together around specific topics related to the model and its goals, working collaboratively to understand, try out, and evaluate strategies and approaches for finding and nurturing exceptional talents in students from typically underserved groups. They identify sources of data to examine for evidence of progress or areas of need, and provide support for one another.

Coaching

Another approach that emphasizes the relationship-building aspect of professional learning is to employ a coaching model. This approach may be particularly effective if a school or district has gifted resource teachers whose expertise may be directed toward serving as coaches with classroom teachers working to implement Young Scholars. Coaching is designed to be a supportive partnership; it acknowledges that often the profession of teaching is solitary work that offers limited opportunity for collaboration and constructive feedback, and responds by promoting more active professional conversation around the work and a safe space for teachers to have support for their efforts to grow.

Some specific areas of support that an instructional coach can provide for Young Scholars implementation include the following:

- modeling the implementation of critical and creative thinking strategies and related observation of student behaviors, and then observing and providing feedback when teachers implement the strategies themselves;
- coteaching to support differentiation for advanced learners and needed scaffolding to promote access to advanced learning activities;
- collaborative planning for effective implementation of challenging curriculum with all learners;
- sharing resources that will support Young Scholars goals, with careful curation and consideration of how to encourage use of these resources; and
- facilitating reflective conversations to help teachers think about how to incorporate particular skills and strategies into their long-term "toolbox."

An instructional coach should be someone who not only brings expertise in the relevant attitudes and practices that will support Young Scholars implementation, but also has the potential to be a collaborative capacity-builder for others. In many districts that do have gifted resource teachers, a movement to an instructional coaching role may be a challenging shift of mindset, because these individuals may traditionally have seen their work as separate from what happens in the general education classroom. Further, they may have limited experience with some of the key responsibilities of being a coach, such as mentoring, curating resources to share, and facilitating professional learning activities (Wolpert-Gawron, 2016).

Thus, an effective program for instructional coaching includes at least two layers of need for professional learning. One of these layers is made up of the needs of the coaches themselves, and the other is the needs of the colleagues with whom they work. Coaches may need to examine and unpack their own prior practices in terms of working with colleagues to explore the differences between giving resources to others and saying "do this" versus meeting teachers where they are and facilitating their engagement with new attitudes, approaches, and strategies. A critical mindset is that coaches are not telling colleagues what to do; rather, they are facilitating a reflective process of planning, implementing, and reviewing to promote deeper learning and strengthen instructional practice.

Several districts using such a coaching approach with resource teachers and classroom teachers have articulated their models into focus on collaborative cycles. For example, one model employs a cycle of personalized learning for teachers on topics they have identified for professional growth, followed by planning for how to use new learning, followed by implementation, and then reflection, which is followed by further personalized learning. All of this can be facilitated by a coach working in partnership with the teacher at each stage of the process. Another cycle emphasizes the movement from modeling to coteaching to increasing depth in collaborative planning, implementation, and analysis of approaches to supporting students with deeper learning.

Voices From the Field

When I first arrived as a school administrator at one of my schools, the advanced academic/gifted program was in transition. As measured by grade-level state standards, the school was a high-performing school. Still, there was not much evidence to support whether students had access to critical and creative thinking and rigor beyond state accountability systems. Our leadership team examined the reasons and boiled it down to three key areas—an absence of curriculum materials, the qualifications of the previous resource teacher, and a lack of professional development across the school. Our administrative team knew there needed to be a change. The first step in embarking upon this change was finding a gifted resource teacher who was proficient in identifying students in need of gifted services and using the adopted gifted curriculum. We needed someone who had the people skills to work with adults and students—someone who could engage with classroom teachers, so teachers would be willing to take on new teaching in their classrooms.

We found our resource teacher! Right away, her mission was to figure out what curriculum resources we did have and what resources we needed. She tiered the list of resources to purchase right away and noted ones we could buy over the next 2 years. She started with resources that had the best educational outcome with the most manageable commitment from teachers. She started attending each grade level's planning meeting to listen to their needs and find areas to grow. She would eat lunch with teachers and help them set up their classrooms. As teachers became more comfortable with her, she was able to start the journey of job-embedded professional learning. Sometimes the professional learning would happen informally—a short conversation in the hallway or faculty lunch. It then transitioned into time in team planning meetings, afterschool sessions, coteaching, and coaching. It did not happen overnight because the work takes time and trust needs to be developed to learn, but the time and effort have paid off. Our children have increased their access to rigorous instruction across the entire school in all subject areas. Our conversations have turned to what gifted curriculum and strategies we can use as standard teaching rather than "we will use it sometimes if our other work gets done."

—Megan Tempel-Milner, assistant principal

Evaluating Progress and Growth in Professional Learning

In setting goals for the professional learning component of the Young Scholars Model, school teams and leaders should also establish indicators of progress and growth. A collaborative, ongoing, formative assessment process supports buy-in around shared goals and provides the space to make the professional learning aspect as important as the student learning.

One key indicator of a solid professional learning initiative is the focus of the professional conversations that educators share. Formal and informal discussions among teachers allow sharing of strategies that work and questions that teachers are exploring. Note that one indicator of a *highly functioning* Young Scholars school on the implementation rubric introduced in Chapter 2 is that staff members regularly engage in conversation around culturally responsive teaching practices. Another indicator would be the ways that teachers engage in discussion around recognizing and supporting student strengths. Such conversations as these reflect not only the specific practices that educators employ, but also the mindsets and perspectives they display related to talent development, cultural responsiveness, and other goals of the model.

Another indicator is the level of collaboration that school staff members demonstrate around practices related to the goals of Young Scholars. Such collaboration is boosted by structures within the school that facilitate space and opportunity for teachers to work together—for instance, scheduling that allows teachers to have common planning time not only with grade-level partners but also with resource teachers who might be supporting implementation of model lessons and advanced curriculum. It is also important for teachers to have the chance to observe one another and debrief about what they experience.

Changes in classroom practice are a key outcome for any professional learning initiative. In a Young Scholars school, administrators and lead teachers can look for signs in classrooms of increased implementation of critical and creative thinking strategies and curricular materials designed with advanced learners in mind. Such signs include not only teacher actions, but also the ways that students respond to the learning activities. For example, sustained attention to talk moves through implementation of curricular resources with a discourse focus will be apparent in how students regularly interact in discussions (Gavin & Moylan, 2012).

Voices From the Field

Our school enjoys a wide diversity of backgrounds from socioeconomic to cultural and experienced a few years of struggle to establish the Young Scholars Model in concrete terms despite leadership calls for implementation.

When I came on as principal, I attempted multiple entry points to impact instruction. Our teachers were highly professional and talented, but were very bound to ensuring our diverse population of students would perform well on high-stakes, end-of-year tests. Being driven by tests locked them unknowingly into practices that did not set students up for long-term success or leave room for innovative ideas or a focus on innovation and dreaming bigger through the Young Scholars Model.

We needed an instructional paradigm shift. Together with my Advanced Academic Resource Teacher (AART), we set out to transform to what we knew would be more meaningful for deeper student learning that would be transferrable—a strong focus on concept-based instruction. In our system, AARTs are instructional leaders and coaches for expanding access to rigor and promoting practices like concept-based instruction, which have long been a hallmark of gifted education, but that we know are a solid foundation for learning for all students. My AART joined all of our collaborative learning teams for planning and cotaught with classroom teachers to support job-embedded professional learning using concept-based curriculum from William & Mary's Center for Gifted Education as a model and guide.

By December of that first year, teachers from preschool to sixth grade were all implementing concept-based instruction with such success and surpassed my expectations. Student engagement increased, and teachers' awareness of student potential began to shift. Through ongoing assessments, teachers could see that students with profiles believed to be less successful on standardized tests thrived on meaningful instructional practices based on ongoing, differentiated assessments. Teachers' collective efficacy increased, and the culture of the school shifted from teaching to a test to more inclusive, free, and meaningful instruction.

—Katie Le, elementary principal of a Young Scholars school

As noted previously, effective professional learning initiatives are responsive to the different needs of different groups of professionals in the school context, based on the roles and individual professional progress of the people involved. Similarly, efforts to evaluate and strengthen professional learning should include attention to indicators of growth for different groups and individuals. School leaders might find that some classroom teachers are showing high engagement with Young Scholars, but that counselors do not seem to have "bought in" to the model, and thus the leaders might devote increased attention to planning professional learning efforts tailored to the needs of school counselors.

Planning, monitoring, and evaluating the ongoing professional learning component of the Young Scholars Model requires a commitment from the team to maintain this emphasis as a perpetual and critical area of focus. Supporting sustained professional learning for Young Scholars includes understanding aspects of how adults as well as children learn; recognizing the importance of nurturing a supportive culture for the model; and ensuring that expectations for educator growth are paired with investment of resources.

Entry Points and Growth Edges for Professional Learning

A strong Young Scholars Model may take shape from a grassroots effort, but the true power of the model depends on systemic alignment and coherence. Figure 14 shows some sample indicators that may reveal entry points and growth edges around professional learning as an important component to Young Scholars Model implementation.

Figure 14
Indicators of Entry Points and Growth Edges for Professional Learning Implementation

Beginning Implementation	Developing Implementation	Deep Implementation and Monitoring for Improvement Areas
❧ Some teachers and at least one school leader have engaged in professional learning around the Young Scholars Model to begin forming the model at the local school.	❧ School improvement plans include goals for professional learning to strengthen the Young Scholars Model. ❧ Schools seek out other Young Scholars schools to form loose networks for professional learning around successful practices related to the equity goals of the Young Scholars Model.	❧ The district collects school growth data around fidelity of implementing the Young Scholars Model to determine areas of need. ❧ The district supports networked professional learning for continuous improvement around strong Young Scholars Model implementation in each school as part of district equity goals. ❧ Teachers engage in individual and collaborative goal setting and reflection around professional learning, with support from instructional leaders.

Chapter 6

Partnering With Families

> No school can work well for children if parents and teachers
> do not act in partnership on behalf of the children's best
> interests.
>
> —Dorothy H. Cohen

Collaborative partnerships between schools and families are critical for supporting students' access to appropriate learning experiences, healthy development and growth, and achievement of their long-term academic goals. In schools that are implementing the Young Scholars Model, educators foster and sustain a perspective that parents and families are integral partners in making the model work. This requires active, two-way communication, culturally responsive actions, and concerted efforts to build bridges between home and school. Further, such partnerships are strengthened through professional learning activities that help educators engage actively and effectively with parents and families.

We believe . . .

- Every parent wants the best for their child.
- Diverse parent and community partnerships make a school stronger.
- All students come to school with strengths and talents that enrich the learning community.
- Families are critical partners in creating the school vision/mission and school improvement and innovation plans.
- Some parents may have not had positive school experiences, and it is the job of the school to build relationships in which parents feel valued and respected.
- Engagement does not look the same for each family, and it is important to welcome diverse ways of being part of the school culture.
- Families may not know how to access available school and community resources, and the school can become a hub for supporting families by providing information and access to such resources.
- Educators may need support and guidance in how to work with the families in the school community, and parent engagement efforts are part of a strong professional learning plan.

In this chapter . . .

- We discuss why family engagement is important for the successful implementation of the Young Scholars Model.
- We outline specific strategies that may help to increase family engagement

Although schools can work hard to build a group of committed professionals and provide opportunities that will reveal and develop student talents, partnerships with families are essential for sustaining school efforts and empowering community members. Family partnerships are linked to all four parts of the Young Scholars Model:

Committed Professionals. Building engagement with families is not often a focus in teacher preparation programs. As part of implementing the Young Scholars Model, committed professionals work collaboratively to engage family members and build strong family partnerships.

Find and Identify. Schools invite parent and family engagement as they seek to understand the myriad ways that students demonstrate their talents. School teams invite feedback from families as they learn more about students who are demonstrating evidence of high potential.

Nurture, Guide, and Support. Partnerships with families are important for facilitating students' access to and success with advanced learning experiences. These partnerships also provide guidance and support for both the families and the school. Often the parents of young scholars appreciate guidance in learning and navigating the school system and opportunities for their students. This relationship is reciprocal in that parents provide critical feedback to the system for how to serve the community and connect with diverse families more effectively.

Essential Elements. Professional learning in a Young Scholars school must include capacity building to maximize family partnerships. Schools also examine and evaluate explicit and subtle messages about whether the school environment is welcoming to parents and supports academic connections for families through school-day or extracurricular experiences. With family and community engagement, schools support parent networks and help them connect to community resources that provide opportunities for young scholars outside of the school day.

Conceptualizing Family Engagement

Family engagement is centered around the idea of relationships. Current approaches for strengthening family engagement emphasize shared responsibility, rather than placing the responsibility more heavily onto the school *or* the parent. Deeper collaborative engagement shifts from an older paradigm of "Please come join us at school, so we can be expert and tell you things," to a new paradigm of "Partner with us so that we can be part of your community and work together to support your children in developing their potential." Traditionally, family involvement focused on what the school needed from families: to come to parent conferences, support their student with homework and projects, attend school events, buy wrapping paper, and serve on the PTA. That approach is fairly one-directional—the school says what to do, and parents do it—and is not particularly welcoming, particularly for parents whose own school experiences may not have been positive for a wide range of reasons. It also prioritizes engagement that is based at the school more than the ways that parents and families engage at home.

The old paradigm of family engagement is shifting and evolving to a new paradigm that works toward a two-way partnership reflective of true engagement. In the Young Scholars Model, inviting family voices in support of the whole child and whole family is critical. Families and school personnel work together to provide the access and support that students need to develop their potential. They also work together to serve as advocates for the child. This partnership requires additional resources and information for families. Educators listen to families as they share their experiences and help identify what they need to ensure student growth and opportunity. Evidence indicates a relationship between a school leader's more expansive view of family engagement and the scope of engagement opportunities that a school provides (Hilado et al., 2013). Fostering such an expansive and respectful view is a key part of making the Young Scholars Model work.

The umbrella of family engagement includes a broad focus on the overall community context in which the school exists, with attention to how the school is connected to the community and thus a part of family life even before a student reaches kindergarten. In contemporary views of family engagement, schools are an active part of wraparound services, working with multiple stakeholders, including community agencies. This provides a foundation for shaping meaningful and culturally respectful ways of collaborating with families rather than merely expecting them to show up on the school's terms. Family engagement with schools expands from just considering the months of the year that school is in session and encompasses more of a "cradle to career" lens with a broad focus on services and experiences for students over time. Schools partner not only with families, but also with churches, community programs, and various agencies in finding ways to respond to student needs.

Building Capacity for Family Engagement

Support for professional learning is a critical part of developing family engagement initiatives. Teacher preparation programs have traditionally given limited attention to family engagement (Epstein, 2018; Mapp & Bergman, 2019), and many school educators may approach engagement with families from a deficit mindset, particularly when they are working with families from populations traditionally underserved by advanced academic programs (Blair & Haneda, 2021). This issue may be compounded by the challenge that often these families may have had negative past experiences with schools and limited trust, which may be further exacerbated by the frequent disparity in demographics between school staff and the communities they serve. Such a combination of perspectives is not a good starting point for an authentic, productive, collaborative relationship between home and school.

The Dual Capacity-Building Framework for Family-School Partnerships (Mapp & Bergman, 2019) is one model for examining and strengthening relationships between schools and families by recognizing the needs and strengths among all stakeholders. The model emphasizes striving toward capacity building in four areas for both educators and families: *capabilities* (skills and knowledge), *connections* (networks of relationships), *cognition* (beliefs and values), and *confidence* (self-efficacy). In the context of Young Scholars, the knowledge base might include the tacit knowledge involved with accessing advanced services, as well as the cultural knowledge and practices of the families served by the school. Relevant networks include direct communication between teacher and parent, as well as the other stakeholders in the school and community who are invested in children's education and growth, and how they have opportunities to be connected to Young Scholars activities. Beliefs and values include assumptions about talent development or about appropriate patterns of interaction. Finally, educators and families may all need to build their comfort and confidence about how to interact with each other and share perspectives and goals.

Engaging in capacity building in all of these areas requires conditions that support such growth, including consistent attention to aligning Young Scholars systemically with other initiatives, active efforts to demonstrate culturally responsive practices, and investment of time and resources to sustain connections. It requires school leaders to go the extra mile to recognize opportunities to increase inclusiveness and promote a focus on equity and involvement.

Professional learning opportunities for teachers that center on family-school partnerships are critical. Such learning opportunities should include strong emphasis on self-evaluation and reflection related to culturally responsive beliefs and practices at the individual, classroom, and school level, as well as educators' overall perception of family engagement and its various forms (Herman & Reinke, 2017). It is important for teachers to be able to raise and discuss questions as they engage in a journey toward greater cultural awareness and responsiveness. It is also important for leaders to frame and facilitate discussions to reduce the risk of perpetuating misunderstandings and inaccurate assumptions. Professional learning activities can build understanding and background knowledge about the community, with a focus on improving efforts to welcome and involve diverse voices. For example, helping teachers understand the stages that some immigrant families or families from poverty go through in navigating educational systems will increase the support teachers are able to offer around various needs in the school community. School staff also strengthen their family engagement through efforts to focus on their communication patterns, including modes of communication and even body language, in their interactions with families (Allen, 2009).

Specific Approaches to Family Engagement With Young Scholars

In the planning process for implementing a Young Scholars approach in a school, family engagement should be both a goal and a strategy to support other goals of the model. Planning should include specific activities that involve families as well as approaches for inviting parents to the table as voices in the implementation and evaluation of the model. From the beginning, a school planning team should include questions such as the following in their planning efforts:

- How do staff members define and understand family engagement?
- How are families currently engaged with the school? What are the strengths of your school in family engagement?
- Which families are engaged, and in what ways? Whose voices are heard, and who might be missing?
- What are the tacit knowledge elements that are important for families to know in order to advocate for student needs within the school and district?
- What support structures are in place for making engagement accessible for more families?
- How do staff members and school leaders specifically focus on making families feel welcome in the school and at school-related events?
- What parent advisory activities and groups are available at the district level that might be connections for a Young Scholars parent advisory group?
- What indicators of progress can you identify to mark progress with family engagement?
- What kinds of resources are available for families within the school or easily accessible from the school? What additional resources might families need or want?

Starting from questions like these, school teams can work to maintain a vision of family engagement as a consistent, essential element, rather than an event. Then, even when there is a focus on specific events, the broader scope of ongoing family engagement provides the foundation. Some of the key elements to support ongoing engagement include the following:

- **Multiple modes of communication and translation.** It is important for communications about Young Scholars to be accessible to the families in the community served by the school. That means translating materials into relevant languages as well as using multiple modes of communication, including paper and electronic means.

- **Consistent invitations for ideas, feedback, and direct participation and interaction in planning and implementation efforts.** In general, most of the communication about school programs and activities comes from the school to the home. Concerted efforts to encourage two-way communication about how Young Scholars is working in the school can promote trust and engagement.

- **Active support for parent leadership.** School teams can be working to encourage parent involvement and to recognize and promote parent leadership for various aspects of Young Scholars implementation. At one Young Scholars school, a parent was invited to share with other parents how he supports his child when she comes home from school. He explained that they each talk about their own day, their successes and challenges, and what they might have done differently. The other parents were intrigued with his story and had lots of comments and questions as they went on to share how they support and encourage their children.

- **Consistent mindset for community involvement.** Another important effort for supporting family engagement is an authentic commitment to ensuring that the school is an active partner with other organizations and businesses within the community to support and strengthen opportunities overall for those who live and work there. Further, school teams can support strong community relationships by establishing partnerships with police and other community helpers for events and initiatives that are intended to be supportive and positive within the community. Some of this community involvement can also be useful in helping schools recognize and facilitate family needs around such issues as transportation and scheduling (LaRocque et al., 2011).

Much of what is described here is consistent with efforts to engage families with schools overall and is not specific to Young Scholars. This demonstrates another example of the ways in which Young Scholars implementation should align with overall goals and initiatives within a school and district.

In addition to these efforts to promote and support continuous engagement, school teams implementing Young Scholars also do plan and implement specific events and activities designed to provide parents with information, support, and opportunities for connection. Some of the types of activities for family engagement in existing Young Scholars schools have included the following:

- **Family advisory committee.** Establishing a family advisory committee for Young Scholars in a school or district is an important way of demonstrating commitment to family engagement, inviting and encouraging feedback, and supporting a consistent partnership between home and school.

- **Welcome committee.** School teams might establish a Young Scholars welcome committee designed to orient parents to the Young Scholars Model. Resource teachers and teacher leaders often schedule times when parents can come to school and learn about the opportunities and services that the model provides. In addition, parents of young scholars meet with parents of newly identified children and share how they have supported their children and the value of participation in the program.

- **Family "coffee chats."** Some schools schedule regular, open, informal meetings for families to connect with one another and school staff who are part of the Young Scholars leadership team. These chats might have specific focus topics, linked to such issues as advocating for students, navigating the systems to support access to resources, or responding to students' social and emotional needs, or they might be more open and informal.

- **Orientation to specific academic focus areas within the program.** School teams may arrange multiple opportunities across a year for families to learn more about the academic emphases of Young Scholars and the curriculum that their children are experiencing. These might include overview sessions before the beginning of a summer program, or they might just be part of academic year events that engage families.

- **Direct involvement with academic activities for Young Scholars.** Families may be able to partner with schools and teachers to be directly involved in some of these academic emphases. For example, parents may be invited to chaperone field trips or help with learning tasks in the classroom. Family members may also be guest speakers in Young Scholars classes, sharing their experiences and how they have faced and responded to challenges.

- **Workshops and resources on specific topics.** School teams and the parent advisory committee work together to determine topics related to Young Scholars that would be useful for families and to provide workshops and access to supporting resources. For example, families may benefit from workshops focused on the tacit knowledge of navigating preparation and searching for college. Or a workshop might include demonstration and engagement with a critical or creative thinking activity akin to what students might be experiencing in their classes, so that families may support these types of thinking activities at home. All of these types of workshops can be supported with online or print resources that families are able to access readily.
- **Family resource center.** Schools and families can work together to determine what kinds of resources might be useful for families related to Young Scholars and their children's talent development, and make those resources available through a family resource center. This might be a location within the school or an online resource center—or both. School teams might collect and share some resources but also invite parents to indicate the kinds of things they would find most useful.
- **Celebrations.** One of the best ways to encourage families to come to school events is to ensure that those events include elements of celebration of and for their children.

Voices From the Field

We identify students as young scholars once a year. At this same time, we hold family information sessions. We send invitations a few weeks in advance to ensure we can accommodate translation and babysitting needs. During the presentation we discuss what Young Scholars is, how it is related to our gifted program, why their children were selected, and what services are provided to YS. Because these sessions are held a few months before the summer program, we are able to tell the parents what their children will be studying, explain what field experiences their children will attend, and introduce parents to the summer teacher. We also encourage parents to volunteer on the field experiences and answer any questions they may have.

—Stacy Hayden, former Young Scholars lead for a Virginia district

For purposes of supporting Young Scholars, it is particularly helpful to incorporate an academic tie-in to many of these activities, including modeling and explaining to families about the connections to students' own academic experiences. For many of these activities that do take on more of an "event" nature, there are additional considerations that school teams can consider to facilitate the engagement of families. For example, scheduling these events for times that will be accessible for families requires gathering some input and doing some experimentation to determine best available times. If it is possible to provide child care and/or transportation for these kinds of events, that may relieve considerable burdens for parents. Language accessibility is also a key consideration; having translators available for events with parents may not be possible for all of the languages in the community, but every effort to ensure translation increases the number of parents who are able to participate.

Voices From the Field

On the Thursday night prior to the last day of the summer academy, families are invited to come and participate in a culminating event. The night starts out with a brief welcome and a dinner. After everyone has time to eat, students lead their parents to their classrooms for a student-led presentation. Students will do skits, lead activities, teach games, and share photos and presentations. Translators are provided based on family needs.

—Stacy Hayden, former Young Scholars lead for a Virginia district

Setting Goals and Sustaining Progress for Family Engagement

As teams work to develop initial plans for Young Scholars implementation in a school, family engagement has to be an integral part of the process from the start. The initial plan should include goals, specific activities, and indicators of progress linked to family engagement, and the goals related to professional learning should also include attention to content on home–school relationships. It is important to make sure that the goals are feasible and incremental; note that in the rubric for Young Scholars implementation outlined in Chapter 2 (see pp. 37–40), the scope and depth of family engagement are expected to be developed and enhanced over time. For example, on the rubric, one indicator of a *highly functioning* Young Scholars school is evidence of a strategic plan and measured outcomes for parent engagement.

The Young Scholars team uses identified indicators as ways of marking progress in the school's capacity for family engagement. It is also important to remember that just as students enter a new school each year when they move to a new area or enter kindergarten, their families will also be new to the school and to the ongoing initiatives and programming related to Young Scholars. Thus, there should always be attention to the needs of families with different past experiences of the school and of Young Scholars.

Sustaining progress and enhancing family engagement also rests upon a commitment to listening to the goals families are bringing to the table and responding to their interests and needs. For example, in one Young Scholars summer program supporting students in grades K–2, the school team invited parents to a workshop in which parents reviewed some sample types of resources and prioritized what they felt would be most useful to them. Parents' top three resource interests were information on social and emotional development of children showing advanced academic potential, information on how to support motivation in their children, and access to free materials that would engage and support their children at home.

The Young Scholars team in a school should also prioritize ways of engaging families as partners in ongoing planning for implementation of the model. For example, the team might consider holding workshops in which small groups of staff and families work together to envision next steps and new opportunities for supporting young scholars in a school, perhaps informed by a "design thinking" approach that engages many voices in considering how to define and address problems and opportunities (Rowland, 2016). Further, by strengthening ties with families and developing networks within the community, the school team helps to build trust and enrich cultural understanding for the staff, as well as promoting leadership from families (LaRocque et al., 2011).

Expanding perceptions of family engagement is at the heart of sustaining progress (Hilado et al., 2013). Family engagement must be not just for families who find their way into the building, but an intentional campaign to ensure all families feel included and empowered in public schools. Meaningful family engagement is not achieved by chance, and there are many challenges to address as school leaders engage their staff and community in refining or redefining what parent engagement looks like in their schools. But strong ties between schools and families promote advocacy and access to opportunities for learners, and thus such ties are central to achieving the goals of the Young Scholars Model.

Figure 15
Indicators of Entry Points and Growth Edges for Family Engagement

Beginning Implementation	Developing Implementation	Deep Implementation and Monitoring for Improvement Areas
✌ Families are invited to see showcased student work and presentations. ✌ Teachers invite open communication and monitor successful practices that engage all families. ✌ Teachers communicate to families about student strengths.	✌ Families, including those from historically underrepresented populations (e.g. students from low-income backgrounds, ELLs), feel welcome in the school. ✌ Families report that they hear feedback from teachers about student strengths. ✌ Families feel their input around goals and opportunities for their student are valued. ✌ Families are surveyed about school planning goals.	✌ Families, including those from historically underrepresented populations (e.g. students from low-income backgrounds, ELLs), are partners in setting school goals. ✌ Families perceive the school as welcoming and actively seeking diverse views and ways to increase family engagement and home–school partnerships.

Entry Points and Growth Edges for Family Engagement

A strong Young Scholars Model may take shape from a grassroots effort, but the true power of the model depends on systemic alignment and coherence. Figure 15 shows some sample indicators that may reveal entry points and growth edges around the role of family engagement as an important component to Young Scholars Model implementation.

Chapter 7

Enrichment Opportunities

> What the best and wisest parent wants for his own child, that must the community want for all of its children. Any other ideal for our schools is narrow and unlovely; acted upon, it destroys our democracy.
>
> —John Dewey

Educational opportunities, often in the form of gifted programs and services, play an important role in the journey from potential in childhood to development and achievement in adulthood. There are multiple pathways to expertise, and because talent is developmental and moves from potential at the earliest stage to growing competency and expertise in later stages, it is important that the learning experiences and opportunities change over time to match the student's stage of talent development. For younger children, exposure to various talent domains through enrichment programs is important to draw out talent and potential and to ignite an interest and passion in future possibilities. This is especially critical for children who may have had fewer early opportunities to access talent development experiences because of poverty, language differences, and/or cultural differences. As talent emerges and coalesces, domain-specific programming that builds content knowledge and skills should be provided, and this can include all forms of acceleration and enrichment. For older students, accelerative and enrichment options are appropriate, as well as programming that enables them to work more authentically and deeply in their domain of talent, via apprenticeships, mentorships or other opportunities to learn from experts in a field. Due to individual differences in developmental readiness and environmental supports, schools need a variety of services, programs, and access points for advanced learners, including ones that enable children with well-developed interests and skills to soar ahead of peers as well as ones that provide opportunities for children whose talents are just beginning to emerge.

Access to advanced learning and enrichment opportunities is critical to the Young Scholars Model, and the model is grounded in a recognition that such access is not equitably distributed for all learners in schools. Schools and communities often provide a wide range of enriched learning experiences that happen both during and outside of the school day, but many learners may not be able to access those experiences as easily as their peers. Thus, a central component of the model is a focus on providing young scholars with enrichment experiences both during school and outside of regular school time, with an emphasis on exposure to new learning and ongoing preparation for more advanced academic experiences. The focus on enrichment opportunities not only builds on other key aspects of the model, including using high-quality, advanced materials and engaging families, but also enhances students' experiences beyond the classroom and the school day.

We believe . . .

- ❧ Many families seek enrichment opportunities for their children, but often young scholars are not able to access such enrichment for a variety of reasons. Schools can bridge the gap for these learners through before- and afterschool and summer enrichment opportunities.
- ❧ Afterschool and summer experiences facilitate a focus on talent development and risk-taking that may be difficult to achieve in the more time-bound, standards-based environment of the normal school day.
- ❧ Enrichment experiences for young scholars in out-of-school time provide important contexts for learning for both students and teachers. Students are encouraged to take risks and engage in problem solving and research in a way that increases their self-efficacy. When teachers are successful implementing high-end strategies and practices with young scholars in

the summer, they are more likely to continue using those strategies during the academic year.

~ Effective teachers in afterschool or summer programs become deeply invested in the vision of Young Scholars and are willing to stretch their teaching style to meet students' diverse needs.

~ Interpersonal connections among young scholars, and between young scholars and teachers, are beneficial for relationships, mentoring, and advocacy throughout the school year.

In this chapter . . .

~ We describe some contexts for enrichment learning that extend beyond the regular school day and school year.

~ We outline the combined benefits for student learning and professional learning that emerge from summer school programming.

~ We address some of the emphases that support a more comprehensive learning and growth experience for young scholars.

Enrichment opportunities in and out of school connect to all parts of the Young Scholars Model, with the strongest connections to essential elements and committed professionals:

Committed Professionals. School leaders who are committed to supporting young scholars recognize the need for high-quality enrichment activities that provide background knowledge, skills, and exposure to a broader range of experiences for students. Principals and district leaders are decision makers around allocating support for programs outside the school day and year, and thus they are also important advocates for young scholars and their needs.

Find and Identify. The importance of access to enriched learning experiences is central to the rationale for seeking and identifying students who would benefit from being young scholars.

Nurture, Guide, and Support. Enrichment experiences that go beyond the regular offerings of the school experience are important to promoting talent development in young scholars. Such experiences, in settings such as focused summer school programs, allow students to stretch and grow their skills and abilities, often in a more relaxed atmosphere than the regular academic experience. The content of these experiences also provides young scholars with learning experiences that they may not otherwise be able to access.

 Essential Elements. Many families seek extracurricular enrichment experiences for their students in the summer or in other time periods outside of the regular school day. However, some young scholars may not have the same access to enrichment experiences outside of school as other learners. Through targeted attention to building those types of experiences specifically for young scholars, the school or district can support access and growth.

Enrichment Opportunities as a Focus of the Young Scholars Model

The rationale for enrichment opportunities as a focus of the Young Scholars Model is to promote access to an extended range of learning experiences for young scholars that will support and benefit them as they continue to pursue advanced academic courses and programs. This component of the model comes from a recognition that although many learners pursuing advanced coursework are engaging in enrichment activities outside school, some young scholars would not necessarily be able to access such experiences on their own because of limits on funds, tacit knowledge, transportation, or a host of other issues. At the same time, considerable evidence exists surrounding the benefits of bringing learners (such as young scholars) together for academic experiences in time outside of school (Little et al., 2010; Olszewski-Kubilius et al., 2016).

As discussed throughout this text, implementation of the Young Scholars Model can and should be viewed as integrated with other goals and initiatives in the school environment. Within that frame of reference, Young Scholars aligns with other initiatives to broaden students' learning opportunities beyond the standard curriculum and to extend the educational experience beyond the typical school day and school year. In other words, a Young Scholars school facilitates enrichment opportunities that extend both the *content* of students' experience and the *context* for their learning. These opportunities may include before- or afterschool programs and experiences, special field trips, and summer experiences, among other possibilities. The focus of these may be advanced or extended learning linked to the regular curriculum, topics that go beyond that curriculum, or practical tools and resources to help students prepare for their next steps in learning and pursue college and career readiness.

These activities provide some of the rigorous learning experiences that will prepare young scholars for success in other advanced academic settings, including building background knowledge, developing skills and dispositions, and engaging with academic peers in contexts that promote challenge. In addition, these activities provide a learning context for educators to recognize the high levels with which these students may respond when given access to advanced learning. These kinds of learning contexts also support teachers in engaging in challenge and risk-taking in their instruction because they may not feel the same pressures of time and testing that they do in the regular school day and year.

Contexts and Content for Enrichment Learning Experiences

The Young Scholars Model emphasizes maximizing learning opportunities for students through programming during the school year and the summer and occurring during regular school hours and before or after school. In this section, we outline some key considerations for the contexts of enrichment learning, suggestions for content, and key features of enrichment experiences that enhance the learning and promote student engagement.

Learning Contexts and Logistics

Depending on school scheduling, some targeted enrichment learning for young scholars can occur during the school day, particularly during specialized intervention blocks or similar contexts. Several key considerations in planning for such in-school activities include grouping and staffing. School-day Young Scholars activities can allow these learners to be together and talk about their experiences and how they are using their strengths in response to challenges. Of course, in a well-organized Young Scholars school, the students would already be clustered for much of their academic learning, but an additional space and time for targeted support may be useful. Further, these kinds of school-day activities should be facilitated by teachers or counselors who have engaged thoroughly in professional learning related to working with young scholars and supporting talent development with a culturally responsive approach.

Although many Young Scholars schools do embed enrichment learning for these students into the school day, there are also many examples of how schools have facilitated enrichment learning experiences outside the regular school day. Young Scholars programming has occurred through before- and afterschool activities, Saturday opportunities, and summer sessions.

These programs outside of the school day often provide additional flexibility for teachers and students, but they also require attention to important logistical considerations. Part of the planning for such programs includes examining questions such as the following:

- What administrative support will be available during programming?
- Which teachers will staff the program, and what professional learning supports do they need in preparation?
- What other staff supports are needed (e.g., nurse, counselor, paraprofessionals)?
- What school or other spaces will be used for programs? What other school resources (e.g., library, playground, labs) will be available during program activities?
- How many students will be involved, and how should they be grouped into classes?
- What transportation is available for students?
- What meals are needed?
- What are the individual special needs of students who will be involved (e.g., allergies, Individualized Education Program requirements), and how will they be addressed?

Content and Resources

The logistics of programming in out-of-school time are critical to making it work, but the substance of the program is also a central focus of planning. As described in Chapter 4, a key focus of the Young Scholars Model is the use of high-quality curriculum that reflects attention to the needs of advanced learners; this same focus holds for curriculum used in out-of-school programs. Overall planning for the model within a school should include coordination around curriculum materials to be used in different contexts with young scholars, with attention to what is addressed in the regular academic year context and what might instead appear in out-of-school learning. The benefit is that the combination broadens young scholars' experiences of curriculum that specifically targets advanced learning. Often, programs outside the school day can be the context for implementing resources that just cannot fit into the crowded schedule of the academic year.

The content of programming for enrichment beyond the regular classroom should also emphasize talent development specific to students' areas of strength. Bringing a group of young scholars together for special programming provides a context for them to discuss their goals, the challenges they perceive around pursuing those goals, and the support they need to take their next steps in talent development. In some circumstances, part of the support can include building foundational skills that underscore next key steps in talent development.

For example, a summer school teacher can work with a student showing high potential in one or more areas of mathematics to fill in skill gaps that might have emerged because of family transience and school absences during the academic year; the teacher would use complex and challenging problems while assessing and addressing skill gaps. Alternatively, a teacher might use concepts that are universal in all languages to engage young scholars who are English language learners and help build their confidence and English language skills. Many teachers find that giving ELLs the opportunity to discuss overarching concepts with peers who speak their same home language helps facilitate translation of their ideas into English. After the students have had time to discuss the concept with each other, they are better able to apply and share it in English.

One teacher shared how she was introducing the concept of change to her class. She had several ELLs who spoke Spanish. After sharing examples of change and giving them time to discuss this concept in Spanish, she had them share in English examples of change in their own lives. One student was able to talk about the changes he experienced when his family came to America. He shared how instead of a well, his family now got water from a faucet, and instead of growing their own vegetables, they now went to a grocery store. His ability to connect and share the *change* he experienced not only deepened his own understanding of the concept, but also gave his classmates a new appreciation for the changes that immigrants may experience when they come to America.

Enrichment programming is also supported by a strong focus on technology integration, an emphasis on hands-on learning, and opportunities for student choice. The schedule and program size of activities outside the regular school day can often allow greater flexibility for use of the school's resources, including technology. Students have more opportunity for exploration of topics and issues of interest in depth. Teachers may be able to devote additional time to project work and hands-on learning that is more restricted by scheduling during the regular school day.

In addition to encouraging students to pursue topics of interest through exploration and project work in enrichment program activities, the educators leading these special programs can also embed engagement with local issues that will be of interest to students and support students in making connections with their community outside the school. For example, teachers can take a problem-based learning approach to support students in studying a local environmental or political question, and the students can develop a plan and communicate their findings to an authentic audience.

Voices From the Field

Upper-grade young scholars at our elementary school had the opportunity to participate in a 15-week after-school program thanks to a grant which covered the cost of teacher pay, bus transportation, new technology, and snacks. The goal was to provide a setting for students to nurture their critical and creative thinking through the use of rigorous problem solving and to instill an appreciation of STEAM education through maker-centered learning.

Approaching learning through the concept of systems was key. For the first few weeks, students analyzed systems through reverse engineering and taking apart common household products to explore their parts, purposes and complexities. We then asked our students to view their town as a system to be explored—noting observations and what might be reinvented or redesigned to improve the town. For the remaining weeks, our students worked on solving one problem: *How can we, as town developers, reimagine our housing, waste, congestion, basic services, and outdoor spaces and create a working plan to make our town a more "sustainable" place to live?* Students were then told that their group had to come up with one idea to improve their town, create a prototype, use BirdBrain robotics technology to showcase this prototype, and then present their ideas in front of hundreds of people at a regional Makerfaire held at a local university.

The weeks leading up to the Makerfaire were a blur. Students came during recess to finish their projects in our Makerspace, some students convinced their teachers to let them come during class after they had finished their work, and every Friday could only be described as creative chaos as students excitedly raced to finish their projects. As teachers, our job was to help the kids troubleshoot, but the projects were entirely student led—some students couldn't get their robotics to work, others couldn't get their designs to look the way they intended, and some students had difficulty conceptualizing how to integrate their technology with their sustainability idea. No doubt it was messy and crazy, but students learned what it meant to be a problem solver and to keep working at something until you arrive at a solution.

On the day of the Makerfaire, the excitement was palpable as students (and many parents by their side!) presented their solutions for sustainability. Ideas included underground moveable mixed-use housing, motorized solar-powered trash collectors, solar-powered outdoor recreation centers, and sensory-controlled recyclable containers!

As we look back upon that special 15 weeks, it'd be hard to quantify growth. Sure, we could try to make an argument that maybe the students will be more likely to enroll in STEAM programming in middle school, or perhaps we could draw some sort of corollary to students' standardized test scores, but dispositional growth was what we wanted. How did students grow as critical and creative thinkers, communicators, and collaborators—skills that will prepare them for the future global workforce? Perhaps the most notable growth I witnessed was in students' overall self-efficacy. They had developed agency in this short time, even a sense of empowerment. As one of our young scholars perfectly captured after the Makerfaire: "I really do feel like I can change the world now."

—Jackie Kwon, resource teacher at a Young Scholars school

Additional Key Features

In addition to the focus on high-quality curriculum for advanced learning, programming in out-of-school time should also build in elements that broaden students' opportunities for access and engagement, and also those that promote their readiness for further advanced experiences. Key features include the following:

> **Field trips.** Field trips are an important part of the learning experience for young scholars in programming in the summer and, where possible, in before- and afterschool time. Field trips broaden students' experiences, enhance learning opportunities, and provide access to people and places that students may not have exposure to on their own. Many Young Scholars schools ensure that every summer school course includes at least one field trip experience, along with building regular field trips into after-

141

school programming. Parents are invited to chaperone the field trips, and many parents often return to the parks, wetlands, historic sites, etc., with families on the weekends.

➣ **Guest speakers.** Guest speakers change the dynamic of a classroom experience by introducing new voices and perspectives and giving students the chance to connect with individuals who have expertise in many different areas. For young scholars, guest speakers can serve as role models and concrete examples of the paths students might take as they pursue their areas of interest and talent. Guest speakers also support students in making connections between classroom learning and applications outside of school.

➣ **Authentic audiences.** As noted previously, communicating with authentic audiences can be a valuable way of helping students build connections between classroom learning and the outside world, as well as supporting stronger community connections. Whenever possible, enrichment opportunities for young scholars should include experiences that allow them to communicate their learning to audiences beyond their teacher and classmates.

➣ **Family engagement.** Family engagement is also an important element of programming beyond the regular school day. Engaging families promotes stronger relationships between school and home, as outlined in Chapter 6, and also may help provide parents and guardians with deeper understanding of some of the resources and experiences that will benefit their child's academic growth. Families also represent an authentic audience for events that showcase students' work in special programs; for example, the school might sponsor an "Innovation Fair" to allow students to share their project work, or a "Family Game Day" for families to experience some of the ways that students have engaged actively with new learning.

➣ **Increasing individualization over time.** As students grow and progress in their own talent development pursuits, enrichment opportunities should be responsive to that growth and promote increasing individualization over time. Programs for younger learners might focus on specific curricular content for whole classes of young scholars, and programs for adolescents might move toward tailoring enrichment programs toward mentoring opportunities and individualized or small-group project development. All young scholars should have opportunities to pursue and develop their individual talents and interests, but such individualization becomes increasingly important as students focus their interests and potential paths beyond K–12 education.

Voices From the Field

A major component of advocating for young scholars is affording them additional extracurricular opportunities outside of their school day. In order to further nurture their gifted potential, it is necessary for us to know these students, partner with their parents, and understand their circumstances. Many students do not have access to enrichment experiences for varying reasons. Therefore, it is paramount to encourage them to partake in new experiences that would lead toward development of talent, broaden awareness of future careers, and lead them to become ethical, global citizens. Additional opportunities for young scholars include afterschool programs. These include the formation of afterschool clubs to extend the curriculum through hands-on practicums, where young scholars can identify themselves as practitioners in the field. As a result of active participation, these students consider themselves to be philosophers, Shakespearean thespians, innovators, scientists, and more.

In addition to afterschool clubs, young scholars benefit from Saturday excursions both within and outside of their local communities. When invitations to accompany these ventures are extended to their parents, they solidify parent partnerships between school and home. In many instances, many of our young scholars' families are immigrants who have language barriers and are uncertain about how to navigate activities for their children that are of little or no cost. When parents are included, the value for participation and "the why" increases in all stakeholders. During the excursions, these parents witness their children realizing future dreams and passions—future astronauts, political leaders, community activists. These group excursions broaden perspectives and enable parents of young scholars to create happy memories and seek possibilities for additional ways to enrich their children.

—Denise Meade-Warren, resource teacher at a Young Scholars school

Spotlight on Summer Programming

Summer is by no means the only context for providing young scholars with enrichment opportunities that extend what can be provided in the regular academic day and year, but it is a critical context for this purpose. In addition, summer programs allow an intensity of focus that can be very influential in young scholars' development, as well as provide professional learning opportunities that enhance educators' readiness to work effectively with young scholars in subsequent academic year programming.

One persistent concern in education overall is the so-called "summer slide," or the learning loss that can occur for students over the course of the summer when they are not engaged in daily academic experiences. This issue tends to be more pronounced for students from low-income backgrounds, who may not have the same access to academically relevant learning experiences during the summer as their peers who have more economic advantages. Summer school programs in general tend to focus on academic remediation, providing support for students who struggle with school and may benefit from the added instruction. However, such programs may not be a good match for students who are young scholars. Rather, more appropriate summer programs for young scholars are those that promote advanced learning with embedded attention to skill development, along with the enriching features described previously.

A summer school program provides young scholars with curriculum and instruction that are designed to strengthen basic skills and develop higher level thinking. These may take the form of project investigations, problem-based learning, research, and independent study. The teachers in the Young Scholars schools create or adapt lessons that connect to the students' diverse cultural, ethnic, and linguistic backgrounds. The learning experiences that they provide young scholars promote a climate in which advanced knowledge, understandings, and skills are developed, guided, and supported. The enriched, engaging curriculum includes concept-based instruction, field trips, and guest speakers.

When a Young Scholars team is planning for summer programming, they must give careful consideration to the logistical questions outlined in the prior section as well as to decision making around the curricular focus of the program. A substantial amount of planning for summer programming must occur well before spring of a given school year, particularly developing plans for the location, timing, schedule, and transportation to support families in planning ahead. Some key activities in planning for a summer program are outlined in Figure 16.

The focus of a Young Scholars summer program should be on high engagement and challenge, with emphasis on active learning and content that will solidify prior learning and/or increase students' readiness for the following academic year. Frequently, a Young Scholars summer program may include multiage classes, with students grouped based on evidence of their specific areas of strength, needs, and interests. Many Young Scholars schools tend to employ curriculum in mathematics and science in summer programs and to emphasize extensive hands-on learning. For example, Project Clarion science units, materials from Engineering

Figure 16
Sample Timeline of Major Planning
Activities for Summer Programs

January/ February	☙ Establish location(s), dates, and overall schedule for summer program. ☙ Coordinate with other summer programs in the same location(s) to begin planning for staff, use of space, food services, and transportation. ☙ Identify focus areas and curricular resources for summer program learning. ☙ Collaborate with school teams on identifying young scholars to be invited to the summer program, including newly identified students as well as continuing young scholars. ☙ Determine possible class sizes and overall program capacity based on space and resources available. ☙ Monitor summer program budget details.
March/ April	☙ Provide families with summer program information and registration forms, with details in their home languages to facilitate understanding. ☙ Ensure communication to students and families that Young Scholars summer school is an enrichment experience, not a remedial program. ☙ Begin developing class lists for classes of about 14–18 students, and monitor registration progress. ☙ Begin hiring summer program teachers and support staff.
May/June	☙ Continue inviting students to the summer program and follow up with families who have not responded. ☙ Schedule and implement a summer school information session/orientation for families, including providing childcare. ☙ Procure classroom materials for curriculum implementation. ☙ Engage summer program teachers in professional learning activities, including focus on the curriculum, culturally responsive strategies, and opportunities to plan collaboratively for family communication, field trips, and other key features of the program. ☙ Schedule and plan for "family days" and field trips during the summer program.

is Elementary, and mathematics units from Project M² and Project M³ are frequently used in summer experiences for young scholars.

Use of existing high-quality, challenging curriculum provides a strong foundation for the substance of a Young Scholars summer program. These resources should be paired with a more comprehensive planning effort that includes (a) attention to how the curriculum connects to and builds on existing knowledge, (b) infusion of critical and creative thinking strategies and a strong emphasis on discourse, (c) accommodations for young scholars who are twice-exceptional or ELLs, and (d) approaches to formative and summative assessment that provide needed information but are different from the high-stakes testing focus that often shadows the academic year.

Summer programs frequently offer students an intensity of focus that is different from the academic year or afterschool programs, because larger blocks of each day may be devoted to the specific content of focus. Planning for these programs can take advantage of the more flexible scheduling but should also reflect attention to students' developmental stages, needs for breaks, and opportunities to relax and play. Further, as in the academic year, planning for Young Scholars programming should include attention to family engagement and how families can be connected to summer programming activities.

Voices From the Field

Parent responses to the summer program were overwhelmingly positive—they highlighted the stories and experiences that their children were excited to share with them. Parents saw increased levels of self-confidence as students talked about the STEM challenges they were taking on each day. They heard from their children about career aspirations in response to guest speakers and exploratory activities. Students were so excited to take on stakeholder roles during problem-based learning and to find paths to solve future problems, and parents were just as excited to share back with us. Parents said that students wished school could be like this all of the time.

—Kelley Hyner, former Young Scholars coach

Several examples serve to illustrate the power of the intensity and flexibility of a Young Scholars summer program. One class of young scholars studied the concept of conservation and what it means to conserve nature, culture, resources, and ideas. The students simulated the role of earth scientists as they explored the effects of deforestation on soil erosion. Through experimentation and data collection they learned how trees and plants hold the soil in place and "conserve" it for the future. A visit to a local wetlands park gave them an opportunity to explore the role of the wetlands in conserving the quality of the local watershed. Later in language arts, they read stories from many different cultures and discussed the power of the stories and oral language as a way to pass on traditions and beliefs from one generation to the next in order to "conserve" culture. The students also experienced the power of conserving their own ideas as they wrote and illustrated new knowledge, thoughts, and reflections in a journal or notebook.

The ideas and problem-solving strategies that students learn during summer school enhance their skill as learners and carry over into the school year. Through the summer school experience, young scholars gain important skills and confidence as they create questions, search for answers, and share what they learn through products and presentations that they design. As their confidence increases, their motivation and willingness to take risks increase as well.

A substantial benefit of Young Scholars summer programming is the professional learning context it offers. Teachers who facilitate summer programs must have first engaged in professional learning around the curriculum to be used, culturally responsive practices that strengthen their engagement with these learners, and ways of responding to the evidence of high potential that they see in students. A summer program often offers teachers a lower pressure context for implementing new curriculum, new strategies, or new technology resources than the academic year because the summer context generally has less focus on high-stakes assessments and may have more flexibility in the schedule.

For many teachers, a Young Scholars summer program may be their first experience implementing advanced curricular resources such as those highlighted in Chapter 4. Once teachers see the curriculum in action and observe student response, they may become more convinced of the value and feasibility of such curriculum for the academic year, thus strengthening instruction in both contexts. Moreover, a summer program context allows teachers to build different relationships with students from their academic year connections, but those relationships may carry forward into the academic year as a source of advocacy and support for learners.

The response of the students to the curriculum is also influential in teachers' perspectives on talent development and the importance of giving students access to such learning experiences. The teachers selected to teach in a Young Scholars summer program should be those who are already committed to the goals of the model; their experience may nevertheless increase and enhance that commitment and help them to be strong advocates for these students moving forward.

In addition to the teachers who actually teach in Young Scholars summer programs, other teachers may benefit in terms of their professional learning by visiting and observing these learning contexts. Such observations in Young Scholars classrooms may be paired with workshops for teachers on the key elements of the model, culturally responsive instruction, and the specific curricular resources in use.

Summer programming is a practical, accessible, and valuable approach to providing enrichment learning for young scholars. It adds more of that rare commodity—time—for students to access advanced curriculum, to be grouped with learners who have similar needs to their own, and to explore relevant and rigorous content with the support of professionals prepared to address their talents.

There are a few challenges and potential pitfalls related to summer programming for young scholars, noted here to support addressing them proactively. Perhaps the biggest potential pitfall is that some stakeholders might come to view Young Scholars as a summer program, rather than seeing summer programming as just one piece of a more complex model. A smaller number of school personnel would be involved in summer programming just by its nature, and that may affect the degree of schoolwide commitment that carries through into the academic year. To address this, it is important for the Young Scholars team to share summer stories and successes with the larger staff in the fall and offer next steps in terms of advocacy and student support to teachers for the upcoming school year.

Evaluating Enrichment Opportunities

A Young Scholars planning team at the school or district level should consider key metrics for evaluating enrichment opportunities along with the rest of the implementation of the model, including initial and ongoing assessment of needs for such programming as well as the effectiveness of implementation of their activities. Evaluation at the initial stage might be guided by questions such as the following:

- What access do different populations in the school or district have to out-of-school enrichment opportunities?
- Does the school or district have a commitment to afterschool or summer experiences for students from underserved populations who are not struggling academically?
- What resources are available within the district for school leaders to access for summer or afterschool program planning?

During and after implementation, the Young Scholars team might examine some of these data sources for evaluation purposes:

- attendance and participation rates of young scholars,
- teacher feedback,
- parent feedback,
- parent and family engagement in special activities during the program (e.g., family day during a summer program),
- teacher use of curriculum and strategies from enrichment programs in the regular academic year, and
- ongoing engagement of young scholars in enrichment experiences.

Resources to Support Enrichment Programming

One of the central challenges for schools trying to implement enrichment programming for young scholars, particularly in out-of-school time, is finding resources—specifically, finding funding to support programs. There are many expenses involved in programs that go beyond the school day, including funding for teaching and support staff, transportation, and curricular resources. This is part of why the schoolwide commitment and consistent support from leadership at the school and district level are so critical for effective Young Scholars implementation; these kinds of learning opportunities are essential for students to make the most of their potential as they progress through school and engage in increasingly challenging academic experiences.

Some schools find creative ways to gain additional funding for enrichment experiences for young scholars by thinking about how the model fits with other programs and initiatives. For example, in many situations Title I funding may be used to support such programs. Young Scholars programming in out-of-school time should be considered within the broader context of other programs to be held in such contexts in order to maximize the deployment of administrative and resource staff. Further, the services to be provided for young scholars may provide a strong basis for connecting with outside organizations that can support enrichment learning for students. Many nonprofit organizations and companies are supportive of educational experiences for learners from economically disadvantaged populations and may be able to provide grants and resources for schools implementing summer and other out-of-school time learning.

Intersection With Other Programs and Opportunities

The focus of the Young Scholars Model on enrichment opportunities during and outside the regular school day supports exploration of connections with a variety of other initiatives, programs, and organizations. Once again, a critical part of effective implementation of Young Scholars is the integration of this focus with other goals and initiatives within the school district. Thus, for example, if Young Scholars is being spearheaded by a district office focused on gifted/advanced learner programs, that office should be coordinating with offices that focus on college and career readiness to explore what opportunities both offices can provide to support learners.

One well-established program that reflects similar goals and approaches to Young Scholars is the AVID (Advancement Via Individual Determination) program, which is oriented toward helping students who show academic promise but are not at the highest levels of achievement in their study skills and preparation for college. Similar to Young Scholars, AVID frequently engages students from backgrounds traditionally underserved by advanced academic programs, including those students who might be the first in their family to attend college. In a district that already implements AVID, there is a natural partnership between a Young Scholars initiative and the AVID program.

Similarly, prior chapters have emphasized the importance of partnering between a Young Scholars leadership team and content-area leaders within a school district. These partnerships can be beneficial for enhancing enrichment opportunities through efforts to collaborate around curricular areas of focus, showcases of student work, and professional learning, because there may be valuable alignment across multiple programs being planned for summers or afterschool experiences.

Entry Points and Growth Edges for Enrichment Opportunities

A strong Young Scholars Model may take shape from a grassroots effort, but the true power of the model depends on systemic alignment and coherence. Figure 17 shows some sample indicators that may reveal entry points and growth edges around enrichment opportunities as an important component to Young Scholars Model implementation.

Figure 17
Indicators of Entry Points and Growth Edges for Enrichment Opportunities

Beginning Implementation	Developing Implementation	Deep Implementation and Monitoring for Improvement Areas
∼ The school provides some before-school, afterschool, and summer options within the school.	∼ The school system organizes summer enrichment opportunities to support young scholars. ∼ Schools provide before- and afterschool options within the school that add enrichment opportunities. ∼ Schools seek community resources that bring connection and inspiration to students about possible career pathways and mentorships.	∼ The school district assesses areas of need and aligns resources to support enrichment opportunities. ∼ Enrichment opportunities are in periodic doses sufficient to influence both student and family enrichment. ∼ Enrichment options include both within-school opportunities as well as opportunities that bring the outside in and take students and/or families beyond the school boundary.

Chapter 8

Expanding the Young Scholars Model to Other Schools and Districts

Young Scholars began as an initiative in a small number of schools committed to the vision and goal of increasing equity and access to advanced learning for students in groups often overlooked by gifted programming. In most districts that have implemented the Young Scholars Model, initial efforts have tended to focus on the elementary level. School teams have used the model as an approach to address identification and service issues in the elementary grades, generally in a small number of schools as a starting place.

Once a few sites are established as Young Scholars schools, district leaders then consider how to expand to a broader range of schools by increasing the number of elementary schools involved and/or by expanding the model to the secondary level. An established Young Scholars school can serve as a model, partner, and leader for other schools beginning to implement the model. Districtwide efforts to support young scholars align with other initiatives promoting equity and excellence, and broader involvement of leaders at the district level promotes consistency and collaboration with other school programs. The expansion of the model to other districts promotes both collaboration across districts and tailoring the model to the specific needs of individual communities.

We believe . . .

- ➣ A pathway for continuous academic growth with attention to all stages of child development from grades K–12 reduces the risk of lost potential.
- ➣ Networking across multiple schools and districts strengthens professional practice.
- ➣ Scaling up the model across schools and districts requires reflection on how to hold key elements of the model consistent while tailoring aspects of the work to the needs of individual school communities.
- ➣ A focus on continuous improvement sustains commitment and promotes effective implementation of the model over time.

In this chapter . . .

- ➣ We address considerations for maintaining the integrity of the model when expanding it beyond one site, level, or district.
- ➣ We provide guidelines for expanding the model to additional grade levels, with specific attention to expanding from elementary-level implementation to the secondary level.
- ➣ We discuss how to expand the model across a wider number of schools if initial implementation has focused on a smaller group within a district.
- ➣ We share observations from other implementation efforts related to the model, with focus on research initiatives that examined aspects of the model's effectiveness.

As with previous chapters, this emphasis on expanding and scaling up reflects attention to all parts of the model:

Committed Professionals. Educators who have been involved with the implementation of Young Scholars, along with their students and other stakeholders, are the best ambassadors for supporting expansion of the model to other schools and districts. District and school leaders facilitate networking and growth for implementation of the Young Scholars Model.

Find and Identify. Expanding the implementation of the model increases opportunities for recognizing and developing student potential. Some students may not begin showing their advanced academic potential until middle school or later. In addition, potential Young Scholars may enter the school district at any grade level. The expansion of the Young Scholars Model to the secondary level responds to the need to watch for and support emerging talent at all ages in students' school experience, and to ensure that students new to a school or district are not overlooked.

Nurture, Guide, and Support. When districts choose to expand the model to additional grade levels and schools, more students are able to access the support and opportunities central to Young Scholars implementation. Further, developing secondary implementation of the model promotes a consistent message with advocacy and support for students across multiple years.

Essential Elements. Scaling the model to a larger number of schools, grade levels, or districts requires coordinating and planning at a central level with involvement of stakeholders across all relevant contexts. Scaling the model up also helps to increase the likelihood that it will remain a priority for the district over time to promote sustainability. The scaling up also increases the demands for professional learning and for resources to incorporate aspects of the model during the school day and in out-of-school time.

Important Considerations in Expanding the Model

Expanding the Young Scholars Model to more levels, more schools, or more districts requires attention to the same considerations for quality that we have addressed throughout the book. These considerations apply whether the focus is on expanding to build a network of Young Scholars schools across a district, articulating the model to the secondary level, or connecting with external partners. Several key considerations to frame plans for expansion are highlighted.

Goal-Oriented and Aligned

Efforts to expand the Young Scholars Model should include a diligent planning process during which stakeholders stay centered on key goals. This attention to goals requires examining the goals that are specific to Young Scholars and how they align with broader goals for the school and district. School leaders, including principals, teachers, and others who are seeking to implement Young Scholars within a new building, need opportunities to understand the model and to see its potential for alignment with other efforts going on at the building and district level to support students.

For example, a broader district focus on equity of opportunity for all populations embraces the goals and vision of the Young Scholars Model, as it ensures access to advanced learning for every student who has the potential to succeed. Another group that is often overlooked for advanced learning experiences are twice-exceptional students. These students are more likely to be identified and nurtured through the portfolio approach that is a hallmark of Young Scholars identification. Similarly, a district that is trying to emphasize increased attention to critical thinking, creativity, and communication skills for all students can be an environment ripe for Young Scholars implementation because the model also prioritizes instruction supporting these goals.

Stakeholder Involvement

Successful implementation of the Young Scholars Model requires commitment and buy-in from all stakeholder groups involved, including school leaders, teachers, counselors, parents, students, and others who are involved in promoting students' growth and development and supporting their access to appropriately challenging learning experiences. The original model was embraced and promoted by a school superintendent. Although the superintendent did not make the model a requirement for all schools, this endorsement immediately made the model a high-profile priority for schools willing to implement new ideas.

Expanding the model also requires building support from new stakeholders, including consideration of the needs of students and those who work with them in different contexts. For example, although school counselors should be a part of

Young Scholars implementation at every level, there are different considerations for counselor involvement when it comes to planning for secondary school implementation as compared to elementary implementation. At the elementary level, counselors are more likely to provide social-emotional support. At the secondary level, in addition to the social-emotional support, they also help to ensure that young scholars are enrolled in advanced coursework and that they have access to college and career planning experiences. In another example, although all schools should involve resource teachers and other personnel in planning and implementing Young Scholars, schools with higher populations of English language learners have an increased need for involvement of ELL specialists compared to schools with different demographics.

Promoting stakeholder involvement includes efforts to inform and engage individuals who will be part of the scaling-up process. Some key informational efforts might include the following:

- Provide clear overview materials about the model, including online information, paper materials, and informational activities, such as in-person sessions and video recordings. Such materials should be accessible for people of different language backgrounds and should limit educational jargon.
- Maintain up-to-date resources about implementation initiatives and student-focused activities, including calendars of meetings and due dates, details of progress toward key goals, and information about student and family programs in out-of-school time.
- Communicate professional and family learning opportunities and priorities by announcing scheduled workshops or other events through multiple means.
- Share experiences and reflections on prior implementation of the Young Scholars Model, including video and written stories from young scholars and other stakeholders at schools already implementing the model.
- Publicize successes and accomplishments related to the model, including sharing of stories about the experiences of students during special programs. Many schools make use of social media, websites, and newsletter as ways of sharing with stakeholders about the work of the young scholars and the teams supporting them.

Engagement efforts may overlap with the informational resources but should also give specific attention to the following considerations:

- Make a concerted effort to invite input and feedback throughout the planning process from multiple stakeholders, including written and oral communication outlets, focus groups, and other activities. Ensure that there are ongoing formative evaluation opportunities as well, with active efforts to invite feedback and new ideas.

ɤ Provide and publicize opportunities for leadership in Young Scholars activities, including roles for school staff and parents.

Focus on Communication, Awareness, and Attitudes

Successful expansion of the Young Scholars Model, like successful initial implementation, requires concerted efforts to increase awareness of the need for and the potential of the model to achieve shared goals for student support and success. It is important for school leaders to ensure communication with all stakeholder groups through a variety of channels, with a focus on building awareness and empowering individuals to play a part in making the model work.

Further, as part of the process of bringing together stakeholders and examining the alignment of Young Scholars programs with existing goals and initiatives, it is important for leaders to explore stakeholder attitudes and support the people involved in trying to initiate the model. Some may be more enthusiastic than others; however, we have noticed that as more and more educators discovered exceptional potential using alternative assessments, those who were skeptical or reluctant soon were convinced and joined the effort.

Voices From the Field

Starting small: I often give presentations on our implementation because I think the Young Scholars Model is powerful. But when you are just starting out, it can be overwhelming, and I want to share our experience and lessons learned with other district leaders. One of the biggest points I try to ensure people walk away with from my presentations is that you need to start small.

We started small in several ways. First, we began working with two schools based on principal interest. One thing we learned was that administrator buy-in was vital. Instead of the district deciding which schools needed the model the most, principals were asked if they were interested, and those were the schools that were selected. We also decided to allow principals to determine which grade level they wanted to start identification with. One school decided to start with rising grade 3 through grade 5 students. The other school decided to start with rising grade 2 students. The administrators at these schools were partners in all decision making during the implementation. They knew what their schools needed, and it was important we gave them autonomy.

Because the program was in a pilot year, this also meant we were starting small with the number of students identified. There was a limited budget in place for the summer program. The team had difficult discussions about which students lacked the three As (i.e., advocacy, access, and affirmation) and selected the students who would benefit from services the most. We decided to monitor the other students and identify more students as we could.

The final way we started small was by only focusing on the summer program that first year. We planned and held a successful 3-week summer program. After that summer, we were able to start providing professional learning to support teachers in serving their students during the year. We were also able to internally evaluate our implementation to date and determine what next steps to take.

Now that the model has been in place for about 7 years, we have made changes. The model is finally implemented in all 14 elementary schools in the district. We have services in place for middle school young scholars. We work on providing professional learning and school year services to identified students. And we are still working on improvements to our implementation and will continue to do so into the future.

—Stacy Hayden, Young Scholars lead in a Virginia district

Data-Based Decision Making

Efforts to expand Young Scholars to more grades or schools should be grounded in the evidence of what has worked previously, both in local implementation of the model and in the broader use of the model across the country (Horn, 2018). Further, planning efforts should include attention to how a school team will monitor progress and evaluate the implementation of the model in the local context. The rubric introduced in Chapter 2 is a useful tool for monitoring progress at different stages of implementation of the model.

Once a school district has implemented the Young Scholars Model in one or more schools, one of the approaches to expansion is to invite other schools to implement as well. Educators can collaborate on multiple levels to ensure that all stakeholders stay committed and informed. For example, the principals of Young Scholars schools may meet once a quarter to share and exchange ideas and challenges for model implementation. Teacher leaders may also join these meetings and/or have their own separate meetings designed to share and explore what works and what problems they have encountered and solved.

In the original implementation of the model, after a pilot in one school, the model was expanded 12 schools. Following that, the district offered the opportunity for additional schools to choose to implement the model if they wished. It began as a grassroots effort led by educators who were committed to increasing access to advanced academic programs for children from groups that were historically overlooked. The success of the model in the pilot schools convinced other school leaders of the efficacy of the model (Horn, 2018).

Supporting implementation in other schools at the same level requires attention to how the model should look similar and how it might be different in different contexts. A central feature of the model is the importance of tailoring it to the context, values, and culture of individual school communities, while still maintaining a focus on the major elements for the sake of fidelity to the model. Every school uses alternative assessments to identify and provide access to advanced learning for young scholars, nurtures and affirms their potential through a high-end curriculum, and becomes an ongoing advocate for their continuous academic development and success.

Although the grassroots emergence of the model serves to ensure initial commitment and staff ownership, sustaining the culture as new leaders transition into schools is critical for continuity. Once the model is established, school leaders should share their plans, goals, and actions with new administrators so there will be a seamless transition and continued support of this important work.

Voices From the Field

The Young Scholars Model is a game changer for talented students from underrepresented populations. I have experienced its impact firsthand as a full-time Advanced Academic classroom teacher and later as an Advanced Academic Resource Teacher. After I moved from Virginia to Minnesota, I had the unique opportunity to teach within a different Young Scholars Model as a gifted specialist. I have since transitioned to an elementary gifted services coordinator role in a neighboring Minnesota district where Young Scholars was not yet in place. Propelled by the strong support of district leaders, I now find myself coleading the implementation of this valuable approach.

How to begin? My first year in the district, I noted that our student population was somewhat socioeconomically and ethnically diverse, but our gifted programs were not. The author of the book *Waking Up White*, Debby Irving, visited our school division that year, and during the Q&A opportunity, a teacher remarked that our school-within-a-school gifted program was predominantly White, while the rest of that elementary building had a large Latinx population. She wondered what caused this disparity. Her comment spurred meaningful discussions among our gifted staff, other educators, and leaders around our perceived "gifted gap." I was glad that we were starting to talk so openly about the racial disparities in our gifted programs, but felt that we weren't ready to launch an approach like Young Scholars quite yet. The following school year, our Gifted Advisory Council, with a healthy membership of parents, gifted specialists, administrators, and Board of Education representatives, selected equity as a topic to be explored. This was our chance to move forward. With the help of the Director of Data Analytics and Dr. Scott Peters's resources for calculating "Representation Indexes," our advisory council was able to clearly articulate the racial and socioeconomic gaps in our gifted programs. The question kept emerging, "How do we fix this?" After we studied the National Association for Gifted Children's (NAGC, 2011) position statement "Identifying and Serving Culturally and Linguistically Diverse Gifted Students," I shared about my experiences with Young Scholars. They were interested, and this discussion moved on to our other gifted education group made up of teachers and administrators, the Gifted Steering Committee.

Now what? The momentum was palpable in both the Gifted Advisory Council and the Gifted Steering Committee. The next step: funding. We needed dollars for an additional position and for curriculum materials, and my gifted budget could not provide this. I wondered how other school divisions with Young Scholars found the finances. Activating my professional networks, I found out everything I could from other coordinators, and ultimately pursued a partnership with our Equity Department as an avenue for creating a Young Scholars position. Because our Equity/AVID Coordinator was a member of both of our district's gifted education groups, she had heard the gifted equity discussions and knew that I had experienced success in other districts with the Young Scholars Model. Fast-forward several months, and we are hiring a half-time position for this as a start. After consultation with other Young Scholars districts, we have decided to focus initial implementation on grades K–2 at two of our eight elementary schools.

How do we plan to ensure success? The Equity/AVID Coordinator and I have built a strong Young Scholars Planning Team, including our Director of Elementary Teaching and Learning and the Director of Data Analytics. In the words of the Elementary Director, we "have the right people on the bus." During meetings, we have open, candid discussions about possible roadblocks and how to avoid them. The Communications Department has supported our efforts by creating professional-looking flyers for communicating and educating our stakeholders. We are off to an encouraging start, and continue to rely on one another for honest, open conversations and trouble-shooting. With this team, and the continued support of our fellow Young Scholars school divisions, I am confident that the Young Scholars Model will be a game changer for our Latinx, Black, and economically diverse students whose high potential is there and ready to be nurtured!

—Molly Hammel, gifted program coordinator in Minnesota

Young Scholars in Middle and High School

As young scholars grow beyond the elementary level, it is important to consider how best to continue providing ongoing support and advanced learning opportunities for them. Thus, districts may work to develop vertical articulation plans and strategies for young scholars' support at both middle and high school. These plans should include continuous advocacy for young scholars as they transition from elementary to middle and from middle to high school.

Adolescence is a critical time in both brain development and identity formation. Middle school and high school are critical junctures that require supportive pathways for young scholars. Expanding the Young Scholars Model to the secondary level requires some similar and some different types of questions and considerations compared to elementary level implementation.

For example, identification for advanced programs may be a different process at the middle and high school levels. Some schools have an open enrollment process for advanced courses that allows students to register in their areas of strength, while others continue a formal identification process that limits who participates. In addition, students' social and talent development areas may shift in focus, influencing the type of interventions that are age-appropriate and applicable to changing needs. Also, secondary school structures including academic advising, faculty relationships, and extracurricular opportunities change from the elementary level. Further, the approaches to grouping in general and bringing young scholars together as a community look different at the secondary level. All of these considerations support the need to code young scholars in district records throughout their school careers so that counselors and educators can be aware of them and continue to advocate and provide access to learning opportunities that will support their talent development.

Assessing School Culture

If the Young Scholars Model is new to a school, it will be important for the team leading model implementation to assess the school culture for the type of professional learning opportunities that may be needed. Such an assessment is important for any school implementing the model, but there are particular assessment elements that have increased relevance at the secondary level. An assessment of school culture and readiness for the model will help to ensure that the mindsets and actions of school staff are focused and aligned with talent development for all students. It will also allow a school to offer different professional learning opportunities tailored to the needs of individual educators. Overall, these assessments help to ensure that educators are knowledgeable about how to support and achieve the Young Scholars Model outcomes.

Helpful assessment questions the team might consider include the following:

- Have school leadership and school staff created and articulated a vision that includes a belief that all students have a profile of academic strengths and that all students should have access to advanced coursework in one or more subject areas?
- Are administrators intentional about using hiring practices and assigning school leadership roles to include diverse voices and perspectives?
- What professional learning has been provided to staff to help them understand the Young Scholars Model and specific strategies for supporting the success of students from historically underrepresented groups in advanced coursework?
- Is there a structure for ongoing professional learning and continuous improvement around deeper learning for all students and the tenets of rigorous instruction?
- Is there a structure for staff input and collaboration around increasing access to advanced coursework for underserved groups of students?
- Are there structures for consistent and targeted data evaluation that informs school goal setting and improvement?
- Is the master schedule designed to maximize student opportunities and ensure scheduling conflicts are not barriers to student access?
- Is time for support built into the calendar (e.g., an intervention block that can cluster group young scholars with a teacher who can mentor for specific conferring or group lessons)?
- What are some possible contexts and structures for bringing young scholars together as a community, and what needs are there for additional contexts and structures for this purpose?

The Role of the School Counselor

School counselors should be a part of Young Scholars implementation at all levels from grades K–12, but they serve two particularly focused roles at the middle and high school levels. First, they serve as important advocates in academic advising and can provide social-emotional and academic check-ins to ensure success in advanced coursework. Second, because of their continuous relationship with the student, they also provide a hub for connecting the many teachers with whom the student will interact.

During academic advising, school counselors meet individually with students to discuss upcoming course selections. Multiple data points are used in the conversation, including student academic and career goals, achievement in current courses, and interest areas. As part of their support for young scholars, it is important for counselors to talk with students about their strengths and how they use those strengths in response to challenges.

The following questions may be helpful to support the academic advising process:

- Which classes have you enjoyed the most this year, and what was it about them that you liked?
- Tell me about your aspirations and hopes.
- What do you identify as your strengths and assets?
- How would you like to push yourself to grow in the coming semester?
- What strategies have you used to manage your time?
- What strategies have you used to stay organized?
- What do you typically do when challenges arise?
- Which (honors, AP/IB, advanced) courses do you plan to take in the coming year?
- What do you think you'll need in order to be successful? What can I do to help?

Voices From the Field

Maintaining the identity of young scholars as they grow into different levels of school and development is important. Without intentional focus, not all young scholars confidently continue in their scholarly identity, so we have made it our goal to reintroduce our scholars to the Young Scholars Model and what that means for them as they grow into adulthood. At our high school, we strive to bring our young scholars together, creating a community in which young scholars work and support each other. Our students not only identify as young scholars, but also access the supports available to help them reach their individualized goals.

As Young Scholars advocates and educators, we must first build effective relationships with our students. Our students will not work with us if they do not know or trust us. Additionally, as a school with a high number of identified young scholars (23%), addressing each student by name and by need is daunting, but it can be done through cohorting young scholars in grade-level advisory sections and by incorporating the Young Scholars culture in Tier 1 instruction, student activities, academic advising, conferences with counselors, and discipline with administrators. All stakeholders connected to that student use common Young Scholars language when working with and supporting the scholar.

Secondly, an essential element to fully support Young Scholars culture must include commitment and understanding of the Young Scholars Model as a school staff. Cultivating common language, skills, and resources needed to assist all educators on the staff as they support students to access rigorous curriculum and systems of support is imperative.

As students grow up, it is natural that some may lose awareness of what it means to be a young scholar. We have seen young scholars in this situation who were not taking advantage of our enrichment opportunities begin to reconnect to their Young Scholars identity when coaches started to speak to them as young scholars, administrators and counselors reaffirmed high expectations, and teachers embraced an equity lens to rigor through access to advanced courses coupled with thoughtful scaffolds.

—Sarah Freeland, high school English teacher

Strategies to Support Social-Emotional and Academic Growth for Young Scholars at the Secondary Level

The school leadership team should assess the types of supports in place not just to have students enroll in advanced coursework, but also to provide proactive supports that set young scholars up for success in those courses. Some categories and examples of support are outlined in Figure 18. Highlights from specific schools that have built supportive experiences for young scholars at middle and high school are described in the following paragraphs.

Midquarter Academic Advising Weeks. One middle school has school counselors meet with students quarterly to monitor progress in higher level

Figure 18
Categories and Examples of Proactive Supports

Relationship Building	Transitional Supports
≈ Mentoring programs with older young scholars ≈ Mentoring programs with teachers in academic interest areas ≈ Cluster grouping and attending to feelings of belonging ≈ Summer programs ≈ Positive teacher feedback ≈ Emphasis on growth mindset	≈ Vertical articulation meetings at transition from elementary and transition to high school ≈ Vertical articulation between grade levels ≈ Orientation visits and early start opportunities
Academic Supports	**Enrichment Opportunities**
≈ Afterschool programming ≈ AVID ≈ Scaffolding for language, executive functioning, or study skills ≈ Cluster grouping young scholars and attending to student identity ≈ Infusion of growth mindset philosophy in curricular units and projects	≈ Summer programs ≈ Afterschool programming ≈ University partnerships for mentoring, courses, or special programs

classes. Young scholars receive time-stamped, individualized passes to meet with their counselors during the existing intervention block. During the meetings, the counselor and student review the student's current grades, celebrate successes with discussion of strategies and efforts that were helpful in those successes, and make concrete agreements to improve any at-risk grades. All young scholars are expected to enroll in a minimum of one higher level class and earn A's and B's.

Progress Reflection and Goal Setting. Another middle school designed quarterly reflection group meetings for young scholars. During this time, administration and leadership team members visit to ensure frequency of relationship connections and clear messaging about care and expectations. Students have guest speakers or watch short video clips of students from similar backgrounds who are finding success and often face obstacles on their path. Students reflect on three questions: *What can I do to support myself? What can teachers do to support me?*

What can administrators, counselors, or other trusted adults or peers do to support me? The answers to the questions are shared with the Young Scholars teachers to assist in supporting student success.

Freshman 101 Institute. One high school started a Freshman 101 summer institute designed to help rising ninth-grade students feel confident both academically and socially as they begin high school. Teachers help jump-start the year by engaging students in fun and collaborative sessions on topics such as note-taking and study skills, time management, organization, and high school life. Additionally, a group of upperclassmen welcome freshman participants with a student panel, team-building exercises, and other group activities to help acclimate to the new school and build their support network. Although enrollment in the Freshman 101 summer institute is available to all rising ninth-grade students, one of the primary goals of the program is to encourage young scholars to attend.

Peer Tutor-a-Thon. One high school started a peer tutoring center that is hosted once or twice a quarter afterschool for 3 hours to allow students to receive help from peers on either content or study tips. Tutors set up tables according to subject area, and young scholars self-select where they would like to spend their time based on their needs. Several teachers have recently started attending the tutor-a-thons also, which has increased success and awareness of the opportunity in the school.

Advanced Placement Summer Boot Camp. One high school started an annual AP Boot Camp, an interactive leadership conference at which students discuss and practice the skills required for success in AP classes, college, and the corporate world. The program was designed for students who are enrolling in their first AP class in the fall, with an emphasis on targeting young scholars. Program facilitators help students develop five attributes: teamwork, communication, organization, reading, and problem solving. AP Boot Camp actively engages students in the development and use of these skills while demonstrating their importance to AP-level rigor.

Promoting Leadership and Engagement With Young Scholars

At the secondary school level, young scholars themselves should have increasing opportunities to be involved with planning and implementation of Young Scholars programming. School teams may invite students to be engaged as active members of planning and evaluation activities, as well as encouraging opportunities for students to contribute their own ideas and efforts toward sustaining the model in schools.

For example, in one high school, a junior who was a young scholar wrote and received a grant to provide an afterschool program for young scholars at her former elementary school. The money allowed the elementary school to offer bus transportation home for young scholars who stayed for the special program. The students engaged in challenging learning activities that stretched their minds and increased their self-efficacy. Other school districts have high school young scholars volunteer during the Young Scholars elementary summer school program. Teachers greatly appreciate having the high school students guide and support student engagement in the advanced learning activities they are providing, not only because of the extra support but also because the high school students are examples and role models for the younger children.

 ## Voices From the Field

The Young Scholars Model strives to provide opportunities for students to engage in experiences that develop talents that will prepare them for challenging coursework, lifelong positive mindsets, and healthy habits, which propagate integrity. During the most recent changes to delivery of lessons due to the global pandemic, learning is now in a virtual setting. Within synchronous and asynchronous learning environments, it is important to maintain structures that will continue to cultivate caring cultures that value agency, affirmation, self-identity/confidence, flexible thinking, collaboration, and empathy.

One of the modalities for achieving this type of classroom climate is to set a purpose, which helps young scholars to understand that communities are interdependent. They each have an important role, beginning with their classrooms, that extends through a global network. Educators need to make it clear that there is power in students' voices and that Young Scholars is a pipeline developed to ensure their success. In the same light, they must reach back to younger young scholars and advocate for them by modeling compassionate behaviors that would help them to succeed. As a result of building this multiyear network, young scholars would be able to apply the skills they've learned in previous years by facilitating classroom discussions and assuming other leadership roles within their classroom ecosystems. Young scholars can demonstrate leadership skills by collaborating with their classroom teachers during planning sessions, brainstorming project ideas, and preparing and teaching critical thinking strategies. This equitable practice affords students lifelong access to empowerment, self-confidence, empathy and community—all of which lead to the exemplification of global citizenship.

—Denise Meade-Warren, resource teacher at a Young Scholars school

Evaluation and Continuous Improvement Efforts

All schools and districts implementing Young Scholars should engage in a process of continuous self-examination with an eye to strengthening the model and ensuring sustainability. Such evaluation efforts should include a focus on specific outcomes, including such data as the number of young scholars succeeding in advanced courses, being identified for advanced academic services and experiences, and enrolling in higher education. Evaluation should also focus on the internal evidence of support for the Young Scholars Model, including signs of a supportive school culture, engagement with families and the community, and educator engagement in professional learning relevant to the model's goals.

In Chapter 2, we provided a sample rubric for assessing implementation of the model, with primarily an elementary focus. A similar rubric with a secondary focus appears in Figure 19.

Research Connections

Expansion efforts around the Young Scholars Model have included not only broader implementation by schools and districts, but also research initiatives that have examined aspects of the model as part of funded projects in several states. The Jacob K. Javits Gifted and Talented Students Education Program provides competitive grant funding for projects that support identification and services for gifted learners, particularly those from traditionally underserved populations; thus, this program aligns well with the Young Scholars Model. In recent years, the program has funded several projects linked to Young Scholars that have included school district and state-level and university partnerships. These projects have examined implementation of the Young Scholars Model and demonstrated ways of providing external support to study the model's effects on key learner and program outcomes.

Figure 19
Young Scholars Implementation Rubric, Secondary Level

	Launching	Developing	Highly Functioning
	Committed Professionals		
Leadership	• Young Scholars Model is seen primarily as the responsibility of one person (e.g., principal or assistant principal, AP or IB coordinator, school counselor, dean of students, teacher leader).	• There is a designated lead for the Young Scholars Model. • Responsibility for the Young Scholars Model is shared among multiple school leaders (e.g., principal or assistant principal, AP or IB coordinator, school counselors, Director of Student Services, dean of students, teachers). • Many teachers know about the Young Scholars Model.	• A school-based administrator coordinates implementation of the Young Scholars Model with a strategically selected committee (may include principal or assistant principal, AP or IB coordinator, school counselors, Director of Student Services, dean of students). • There is a designated Young Scholars lead for the committee. • There is a specified goal related to Young Scholars enrollment and success in advanced courses as part of a school improvement plan/strategic plan.

Figure 19, *continued*

	Launching	Developing	Highly Functioning
Depth of Understanding	∾ Teachers are developing an understanding of the role of school staff in the Young Scholars Model. ∾ Staff has some understanding of culturally responsive teaching practices.	∾ The school is beginning to set goals around the enrollment of young scholars in advanced courses. ∾ Teachers are becoming informed about and participate in the identification of young scholars. ∾ Teachers are using interventions that support young scholars' success in advanced courses. ∾ Staff engage in conversations about culturally responsive teaching practices. ∾ Schools network with other schools to share strategies to support young scholars' identification, enrollment in advanced courses, and instructional success.	∾ All teachers are informed about Young Scholars, play a role in interventions that support success in advanced coursework, and demonstrate a personal commitment to the support of young scholars in accessing advanced learning opportunities. ∾ Staff routinely engage in purposeful conversations and self-reflection regarding culturally responsive teaching practices. ∾ Schools regularly network and share successful identification, enrollment, and instructional strategies with other schools in an effort to sustain access to rigor.

Figure 19, *continued*

	Launching	Developing	Highly Functioning
		Find/Identify	
Advocacy, Access, and Affirmation	❧ Principal or other Young Scholars leader initiates most conversations about advocacy, affirmation, and access for students. ❧ Most staff are not yet aware of the model, equity efforts around access to rigor, or who young scholars are in their classes or within the school.	❧ Staff are developing an understanding of the Young Scholars profile to include focus on advocacy, affirmation, and access. ❧ Staff discuss students for potential identification as young scholars. ❧ Staff are aware of the proportional representation of subgroups in their classes as compared to the proportional representation of subgroups in the school.	❧ There is a schoolwide awareness of previously identified young scholars, which is used to inform course selections. ❧ Staff actively and routinely search for and identify students not previously identified as young scholars using multiple data points and consideration of advocacy, affirmation, and access. This information is shared with the Young Scholars school team. ❧ Student services teams intentionally use Young Scholars information and data as part of the academic advising process to support appropriate levels of rigor and challenge in course selections.

Figure 19, *continued*

	Launching	Developing	Highly Functioning
Advocacy, Access, and Affirmation, *continued*			೩ Staff actively work to improve the proportional representation of subgroups in advanced coursework as compared to the proportional representation of subgroups in the school.
Advanced Opportunities as an Identification Tool	೩ Staff have limited understanding of how opportunities to engage with advanced academic strategies and curriculum (e.g., critical and creative thinking strategies) can support the identification of young scholars.	೩ Staff are developing an understanding of the importance of aligning a student's access to advanced coursework to their areas of interest or strength. ೩ Some use of critical and creative thinking strategies and higher level performance tasks are used to help identify advanced potential.	೩ Each grade level/department has a plan for routine opportunities for engagement with advanced academic opportunities (e.g., critical and creative thinking strategies) to support and identify potential young scholars. ೩ Schoolwide use of performance assessments that incorporate higher level tasks are used to show student growth and as an indicator of student potential.

Figure 19, *continued*

	Launching	Developing	Highly Functioning
		Nurture, Guide, and Support	
Cohorts	☙ Limited Young Scholars cohort groupings exist.	☙ Young Scholars cohorts are grouped for classes or advisory periods by some grade levels/departments.	☙ Young scholars are strategically grouped in cohorts for classes or advisory periods with teachers who are committed to providing growth mindset culture and "teaching up."
Interventions	☙ Use of advanced academic strategies and curriculum is limited, other than in Young Scholars summer camps, AVID, and other special programs.	☙ Advanced academic strategies and curriculum are occasionally provided to young scholars. ☙ Executive function and college-and-career skill development resources (e.g., AVID, Naviance) are shared and used in classrooms as well as in Young Scholars summer camps, advisory periods, AVID, or other special programs.	☙ Young scholars have weekly opportunities to access advanced strategies and curriculum in the classroom. ☙ Executive function and college-and-career readiness skills are purposefully developed in the classroom as well as in Young Scholars summer camps, advisory periods, AVID, and/or other special programs.

Figure 19, *continued*

	Launching	Developing	Highly Functioning
Monitoring	❧ Teachers monitor young scholars' grades and other academic indicators of progress.	❧ Monitoring of young scholars' performance, grades, and progress involves quarterly check-ins by the Young Scholars team.	❧ Young scholars are monitored monthly for changes in progress, performance, and grades to include quarterly individual check-ins with young scholars regarding grades. ❧ Young Scholars team relays information to teachers and support staff biweekly.
Essential Elements			
Professional Learning	❧ An overview of the Young Scholars Model is shared with staff at some point in the early part of each school year.	❧ Teachers attend at least one of the multiple opportunities for professional learning to support the Young Scholars Model (e.g., courses or workshops, networking).	❧ A designated Young Scholars lead is actively engaged in discussions with collaborative teams and is able to support teachers in advanced strategies and curriculum as an intervention.

Figure 19, *continued*

	Launching	Developing	Highly Functioning
Professional Learning, *continued*			❧ Classroom teachers attend workshops on advanced curriculum and strategies through professional learning days and use opportunities to plan for Young Scholars instruction and interventions with school teams.
School Planning and Vertical Articulation	❧ At least one schoolwide intervention to support young scholars is planned as part of the school schedule or master calendar (e.g., curriculum, summer school, afterschool, family engagement).	❧ At least two schoolwide interventions to support young scholars are planned for each school year. ❧ There is some discussion of how to meet the needs of young scholars during grade-level and school transitions.	❧ Multiple strategic schoolwide interventions are planned. ❧ School counselors and other school staff engage in vertical articulation discussions regarding young scholars during grade-level and school transitions.

Figure 19, *continued*

	Launching	Developing	Highly Functioning
Family Engagement	≈ Schools use translated documents to inform families about young scholars.	≈ Schools use translated documents to inform families about young scholars. ≈ Schools have outreach to ensure that information and curriculum sessions are inclusive and inviting.	≈ Schools use translated documents to inform families about young scholars. ≈ Schools have strategic and measurable goals for outreach to include families in enrichment, advanced programs, and other events highlighting access to rigor.

Project SPARK and Project LIFT

Project SPARK (Supporting and Promoting Advanced Readiness in Kids) was designed to implement key components of the Young Scholars Model in four New England school districts (Little et al., 2018). The federally funded research project was a collaboration between these school districts and researchers at the University of Connecticut and the University of Louisville. These districts had less comprehensive gifted programming than existed in some of the original Young Scholars contexts, but they also had a problem of underrepresentation of particular groups in their gifted identification process and gifted services. In Project SPARK schools, teachers in grades K–2 worked with the research team to find and support students who were demonstrating gifted behaviors, focusing specifically on students from underrepresented populations. Teachers referred students to the project based on these observations, and SPARK students had opportunities to participate in summer programming in mathematics, using units from Project M² (Gavin et al., 2013).

The research team examined mathematics achievement for SPARK students following summer program participation and also explored patterns of identification for local gifted programs in the years following SPARK implementation. Results indicated positive effects of summer program participation on mathematics achievement (compared to similar students who did not participate; Little et al., 2018). Evidence also indicated that teachers in the SPARK treatment schools referred more students from underrepresented groups to the project than teachers in comparison schools, and that higher proportions of students from these groups were later identified for their local gifted programs (Kearney et al., 2019). Thus, the project demonstrated further evidence of the benefits of a Young Scholars approach, both for student achievement and for increasing equitable representation in advanced academic programs.

Project LIFT, a follow-up initiative also funded by the Javits Program, included further focus on engaging classroom teachers in the early grades in recognizing potential and infusing more critical and creative thinking strategies in content-area instruction. Emerging evidence from this project also shows the value of helping teachers think about what academic potential looks like in diverse populations, with evidence of broadening perceptions of behaviors indicating talent (Kearney et al., 2021). Further, classroom observation evidence shows increases in teacher use of strategies supporting critical and creative thinking, particularly around use of higher level discourse in mathematics instruction (Little, 2020).

Project RAP

Another federally funded research initiative, Project Reaching Advanced Potential (RAP) was a collaboration among the Kentucky Department of Education, Jefferson County Public Schools, and researchers from Western Kentucky University and the University of Louisville. Similar to Project SPARK, Project RAP engaged several schools with issues of underrepresentation in their advanced learning programs in implementing aspects of the Young Scholars Model, including the use of response lessons in classrooms to provide the context for teachers to observe students as they engaged with critical and creative thinking strategies. This project also showed results indicating greater diversity in the district's primary talent pool following the implementation of the model (Adelson et al., 2017), as well as broadened awareness among school personnel of how to look for talent potential in diverse populations (Marsee, 2019).

Successful Partnerships

These research-focused projects demonstrate ways that universities and school districts can partner in making the Young Scholars Model work in schools. Some of these projects differ from the original Young Scholars efforts in that they are often spearheaded in large part by an organization outside the school district, and thus they are somewhat less of a "homegrown" initiative. With these types of partnerships, several considerations are key to implementing the model successfully and supporting sustainability:

- Build local support and buy-in. Throughout this text, we have emphasized the importance of a schoolwide commitment to the Young Scholars Model. When the initiative begins outside the school, it may be an uphill battle to build that same degree of buy-in, but local commitment is critical to sustainability.
- Empower teachers to own the implementation. In addition to the schoolwide commitment, it is also important to ensure that there are teacher leaders who take responsibility for implementing the model and feel ownership of its success.
- Develop collaborative relationships that engage the local, situated knowledge of the people who are implementing at the school level. Every implementation of the Young Scholars Model is a little different because by design it is intended to fit within the goals and culture of a school (although it may also bring some transformation to the goals and cul-

ture). This means that tailoring the model to a particular context requires engagement of the stakeholders within that context to promote success.

Expanding Awareness and Outreach

A key part of building and sustaining school programs that support the Young Scholars Program is engaging in active communication and outreach efforts highlighting the model's successes. Inequities in gifted programming receive considerable attention in the press, sometimes with resulting recommendations to cease all special programming for advanced learners. Evidence that shows successful efforts to find and nurture talents in students from underrepresented populations, on the other hand, demonstrates the value of tailoring talent development efforts to the strengths and needs of learners in the community and underscores the importance of ongoing work to support these students. Further, when schools and districts share their successful efforts with the Young Scholars Model, they provide useful details for other schools and districts seeking ways of increasing equitable access to advanced programs.

Awareness efforts can span a wide range of activities. The Young Scholars team for a school or district might include a goal about public awareness, and highlight specific metrics and activities, such as outreach to local press for coverage of Young Scholars activities and initiatives. Newsletters and school websites can highlight programs and activities as well, and these may provide a good context not only for educators, but also for young scholars themselves, to write and share stories about their experiences. Social media also provides an excellent context for a Young Scholars team to share the work they are doing to support and celebrate students.

Final Thoughts

Schools that implement the Young Scholars Model take a comprehensive approach to the issue of underrepresentation that changes the culture of the school and their perception of what children can do. Through shared leadership, collaboration among educators, and ongoing professional learning experiences, teachers gradually move beyond a reliance on test scores and begin to take a multidimensional look at evidence of talent potential through a much broader lens. This includes a review of daily learning activities, performance assessments, and interactions with their students. Teachers, principals, and all school staff actively search for evidence of advanced potential in students who had historically been overlooked. They also involve families in the process and enlist support at home in nurturing the advanced academic potential of these young children. The changes in school culture and the multilayered structures that support a change from within lead to systemic change within these schools that is more likely to endure. Because the problem of underrepresentation is complex, a multifaceted approach with multiple layers of support is needed to implement changes and practices that allow every student, regardless of cultural, ethnic, or linguistic background, to have access to advanced academic programs and learning opportunities that promote continuous academic growth.

References

Adelson, J. L., Snyder, K. E., Pittard, C., Frazier, L., & York, H. (2017, April). *Improving the diversity of the primary talent pool: Evidence from the Reaching Academic Potential (RAP) project* [Paper presentation]. American Educational Research Association Annual Meeting, San Antonio, TX, United States.

Allen, J. (2009, January). Effective home-school communication. *FINE Newsletter, 1*(1). https://archive.globalfrp.org/family-involvement/publications-resources/effective-home-school-communication

Bangel, N. J., Moon, S. M., & Capobianco, B. M. (2010). Preservice teachers' perceptions and experiences in a gifted education training model. *Gifted Child Quarterly, 54*(3), 209–221. https://doi.org/10.1177/0016986210369257

Berger, R., Woodfin, L., & Vilen, A. (2016). *Learning that lasts: Challenging, engaging, and empowering students with deeper instruction*. Jossey-Bass.

Bernal, E. M. (2002). Three ways to achieve a more equitable representation of culturally and linguistically different students in GT programs. *Roeper Review, 24*(2), 82–88. https://doi.org/10.1080/02783190209554134

Blair, A., & Haneda, M. (2021). Toward collaborative partnerships: Lessons from parents and teachers of emergent bi/multilingual students. *Theory Into Practice, 60*(1), 18–27. https://doi.org/10.1080/00405841.2020.1827896

Bracken, B. A., VanTassel-Baska, J., Brown, E. F., & Feng, A. (2007). Project Athena: A tale of two studies. In J. VanTassel-Baska & T. Stambaugh (Eds.), *Overlooked gems: A national perspective on low-income promising learners* (pp. 63–67). National Association for Gifted Children.

Brooks-Gunn, J., Klebanov, P. K., & Duncan, G. J. (1996). Ethnic difference in children's intelligence test scores: Role of economic deprivation, home environment, and maternal characteristics. *Child Development, 67*(2), 396–408. https://doi.org/10.2307/1131822

Castellano, J. A., & Díaz, E. I. (2001). *Reaching new horizons: Gifted and talented education for culturally and linguistically diverse students*. Allyn & Bacon.

Chapin, S. H., O'Connor, C., & Anderson, N, C. (2003). *Classroom discussions: Using math talk to help students learn, grades 1–6*. Math Solutions.

de Boer, H., Donker, A. S., Kostons, D. D. N. M., & van der Werf, G. P. C. (2018). Long-term effects of metacognitive strategy instruction on student academic performance: A meta-analysis. *Educational Research Review, 24*, 98–115. https://doi.org/10.1016/j.edurev.2018.03.002

de Bono, E. (1985). *Six thinking hats*. Little, Brown.

Dike, V. E. (2017). Poverty and brain development in children: Implications for learning. *Asian Journal of Education and Training, 3*(1), 64–68. https://doi.org/10.20448/journal.522.2017.31.64.68

Donovan, M. S., & Cross, C. T. (2002). *Minority students in special and gifted education*. National Academy of Sciences.

Drago-Severson, E., & Blum-DeStefano, J. (2018). *Leading change together: Developing educator capacity within schools and systems*. ASCD.

Durlak, J. A., Weissberg, R. P., Dymnicki, A. B., Taylor, R. D., & Schellinger, K. B. (2011). The impact of enhancing students' social and emotional learning: A meta-analysis of school-based universal interventions. *Child Development, 82*(1), 405–432. https://doi.org/10.1111/j.1467-8624.2010.01564.x

Eberle, B. (2008). *SCAMPER: Creative games and activities for imagination development* (Combined ed.). Prufrock Press.

Epstein, J. L. (2018). *School, family, and community partnerships: Preparing educators and improving schools* (2nd ed.). Routledge.

Evans, G. W. (2004). The environment of childhood poverty. *American Psychologist, 59*(2), 77–92. https://doi.org/10.1037/0003-066X.59.2.77

Ford, D. Y. (2010). Underrepresentation of culturally different students in gifted education: Reflections about current problems and recommendations for the future. *Gifted Child Today, 33*(3), 31–35. https://doi.org/10.1177/1076217 51003300308

Ford, D. Y., Harris, J. J., III, Tyson, C. A., & Trotman, M. F. (2002). Beyond deficit thinking: providing access for gifted African American students. *Roeper Review, 24*(2), 52–58. https://doi.org/10.1080/02783190209554129

Garet, M. S., Porter, A. C., Desimone, L., Birman, B. F., & Yoon, K. S. (2001). What makes professional development effective? Results from a national sample of teachers. *American Educational Research Journal, 38*(4), 915–945. https://doi.org/10.3102/00028312038004915

Gavin, M. K., Casa, T. M., Adelson, J. L., Carroll, S. R., Sheffield, L. J., & Spinelli, A. M. (2007). Project M³: Mentoring Mathematical Minds—A research-based curriculum for talented elementary students. *Journal of Advanced Academics, 18*(4), 566–585. https://doi.org/10.4219/jaa-2007-552

Gavin, M. K., Casa, T. M., Firmender, J. M., & Carroll, S. R. (2013). The impact of advanced geometry and measurement curriculum units on the mathematics achievement of first-grade students. *Gifted Child Quarterly, 57*(2), 71–84. https://doi.org/10.1177/0016986213479564

Gavin, M. K., & Moylan, K. G. (2012). 7 steps to high-end learning. *Teaching Children Mathematics, 19*(3), 184–192. https://doi.org/10.5951/teacchilma th.19.3.0184

Gay, G. (2018). *Culturally responsive teaching: Theory, research and practice* (3rd ed.). Teachers College Press.

Gentry, M., & Fugate, C. M. (2013). Cluster grouping programs and the total school cluster grouping model. In C. M. Callahan & H. L. Hertberg-Davis (Eds.), *Fundamentals of gifted education: Considering multiple perspectives* (pp. 212–225). Routledge.

Haberman, M. (2010). The pedagogy of poverty versus good teaching. *Phi Delta Kappan, 92*(2), 81–87. https://doi.org/10.1177/003172171009200223

Hamilton, R., McCoach, D. B., Tutweiler, M. S., Siegle, D., Gubbins, E. J., Callahan, C. M., Broderson, A. V., & Mun, R. U. (2018). Disentangling the roles of institutional and individual poverty in the identification of gifted students. *Gifted Child Quarterly, 62*(1), 6–24. https://doi.org/10.1177/00169 86217738053

Harradine, C. C., Coleman, M. R. B., & Winn, D.-M. C. (2014). Recognizing academic potential in students of color: Findings of U-STARS~PLUS. *Gifted Child Quarterly, 58*(1), 24–34. https://doi.org/10.1177/0016986213506040

Harris, R., & Reynolds, R. (2014). The history curriculum and its personal connection to students from minority ethnic backgrounds. *Journal of Curriculum Studies, 46*(4), 464–486. https://doi.org/10.1080/00220272.2014.881925

Herman, K. C., & Reinke, W. M. (2017). Improving teacher perceptions of parent involvement patterns: Findings from a group randomized trial. *School Psychology Quarterly, 32*(1), 89–104. https://doi.org/10.1037/spq0000169

Hilado, A. V., Kallemeyn, L., & Phillips, L. (2013). Examining understandings of parent involvement in early childhood programs. *Early Childhood Research & Practice, 15*(2).

Hockett, J. A. (2009). Curriculum for highly able learners that conforms to general education and gifted education quality indicators. *Journal for the Education of the Gifted, 32*(3), 394–440. https://doi.org/10.4219/jeg-2009-857

Hodges, J., Tay, J., Maeda, Y., & Gentry, M. (2018). A meta-analysis of gifted and talented identification practices. *Gifted Child Quarterly, 62*(2), 147–174. https://doi.org/10.1177/0016986217752107

Horn, C. (2018). Serving low-income and underrepresented students in a talent development framework. In P. Olszewski-Kubilius, R. F. Subotnik, & F. C. Worrell (Eds.), *Talent development as a framework for gifted education: Implications for best practices and applications in schools* (pp. 129–152). Prufrock Press.

Isaksen, S. G., Dorval, K. B., & Treffinger, D. J. (2011). *Creative approaches to problem solving: A framework for innovation and change* (3rd ed.). SAGE.

Jacobs, V. R., Martin, H. A., Ambrose, R. C., & Philipp, R. A. (2014). Warning signs! *Teaching Children Mathematics, 21*(2), 107–113. https://doi.org/10.5951/teacchilmath.21.2.0107

Jensen, E. (2019). *Poor students, rich teaching: Seven high-impact mindsets for students from poverty* (Rev. ed.). Solution Tree.

Kaplan, S. N. (2013). Depth and complexity. In C. M. Callahan & H. L. Hertberg-Davis (Eds.), *Fundamentals of gifted education: Considering multiple perspectives* (pp. 277–286). Routledge.

Kearney, K. L., Adelson, J. L., Roberts, A. M., Pittard, C. M., O'Brien, R. L., & Little, C. A. (2019, April). *Access and identification: Gifted program identification following early referral for high-potential behaviors* [Paper presentation]. American Educational Research Association Annual Meeting, Toronto, Canada.

Kearney, K. L., Peters, P., & Little, C. A. (2021, April 11). *Broadening teachers' understanding of high potential* [Paper presentation]. The annual meeting of the American Educational Research Association, Virtual.

Kim, K. H., VanTassel-Baska, J., Bracken, B. A., Feng, A., Stambaugh, T., & Bland, L. (2012). Project Clarion: Three years of science instruction in title I schools among K–third grade students. *Research in Science Education, 42*(5), 813–829. https://doi.org/10.1007/s11165-011-9218-5

Knapp, M. S., Honig, M. I., Plecki, M. L., Portin, B. S., & Copland, M. A. (2014). *Learning-focused leadership in action: Improving instruction in schools and districts.* Routledge.

LaRocque, M., Kleiman, I., & Darling, S. M. (2011). Parental involvement: The missing link in school achievement. *Preventing School Failure, 55*(3), 115–122. https://doi.org/10.1080/10459880903472876

Leithwood, K. (2012). *The Ontario Leadership Framework 2012 with a discussion of the research foundations* (pp. 1–66). Ontario Institute for Education Leadership.

Little, C. A. (2020). *Project LIFT Year 3 supplemental performance report.* Jacob K. Javits Gifted and Talented Students Education Program.

Little, C. A., Adelson, J. L., Kearney, K. L., Cash, K., & O'Brien, R. (2018). Early opportunities to strengthen academic readiness: Effects of summer learning on mathematics achievement. *Gifted Child Quarterly, 62*(1), 83–95. https://doi.org/10.1177/0016986217738052

Little, C. A., Kearney, K. L., & Britner, P. A. (2010). Students' self-concept and perceptions of mentoring relationships in a summer mentorship program for talented adolescents. *Roeper Review, 32*(3), 189–199. https://doi.org/10.1080/02783193.2010.485307

Little, C. A., & Paul, K. A. (2009). Weighing the workshop: Assess the merits with six criteria for planning and evaluation. *Journal of Staff Development, 30*(5), 26–28.

Mapp, K. L. & Bergman, E. (2019). *The dual capacity-building framework for family-school partnerships* (Version 2). https://www.dualcapacity.org

Marsee, M. (2019, April 9). Digging deeper to unearth gifted students. *Kentucky Teacher.* https://www.kentuckyteacher.org/features/2019/04/digging-deeper-to-unearth-gifted-students

Matthews, M. S., & Castellano, J. A. (2014). *Talent development for English language learners: Identifying and developing potential.* Prufrock Press.

Miller, E. M. (2009). The effect of training in gifted education on elementary classroom teachers' theory-based reasoning about the concept of giftedness. *Journal for the Education of the Gifted, 33*(1), 65–105. https://doi.org/10.1177/016235320903300104

Moon, T. R., & Brighton, C. M. (2008). Primary teachers' conceptions of giftedness. *Journal for the Education of the Gifted, 31*(4), 447–480. https://doi.org/10.4219/jeg-2008-793

National Association for Gifted Children. (2011). *Identifying and serving culturally and linguistically diverse gifted students* [Position statement]. https://www.

nagc.org/sites/default/files/Position%20Statement/Identifying%20and%20 Serving%20Culturally%20and%20Linguistically.pdf

Nisbett, R. E., Aronson, J., Blair, C., Dickens, W., Flynn, J., Halpern, D. F., & Turkheimer, E. (2012). Intelligence: New findings and theoretical developments. *American Psychologist, 67*(2), 130–159. https://doi.org/10.1037/a0 026699

Noguera, P., Darling-Hammond, L., & Friedlaender, D. (2015). *Equal opportunity for deeper learning.* Students at the Center: Deeper Learning Research Series. Jobs for the Future.

Orloff, K. K. (2004). *I wanna iguana* (D. Catrow, Illus.). Putnam.

Olszewski-Kubilius, P., & Corwith, S. (2018). Poverty, academic achievement, and giftedness: A literature review. *Gifted Child Quarterly, 62*(1), 37–55. https://doi.org/10.1177/0016986217738015

Olszewski-Kubilius, P., Steenbergen-Hu, S., Thomson, D., & Rosen, R. (2016). Minority achievement gaps in STEM: Findings of a longitudinal study of Project Excite. *Gifted Child Quarterly, 61*(1), 20–39. https://doi.org/10.11 77/0016986216673449

Olszewski-Kubilius, P., & Thomson, D. L. (2010). Gifted programming for poor or minority urban students: Issues and lessons learned. *Gifted Child Today, 33*(4), 58–64. https://doi.org/10.1177/107621751003300413

Osborn, A. F. (1957). *Applied imagination: Principles and procedures of creative problem-solving.* Scribner.

Paul, R. (1993). *Critical thinking: What every person needs to survive in a rapidly changing world.* Foundation for Critical Thinking.

Paul, R., & Elder, L. (2012). *Critical thinking: Tools for taking charge of your learning and your life* (3rd ed.). Rowman & Littlefield.

Peters, S. J., & Engerrand, K. G. (2016). Equity and excellence: Proactive efforts in the identification of underrepresented students for gifted and talented services. *Gifted Child Quarterly, 60*(3), 159–171. https://doi.org/10.1177/00 16986216643165

Peters, S. J., Gentry, M., Whiting, G. W., & McBee, M. T. (2019). Who gets served in gifted education? Demographic representation and a call for action. *Gifted Child Quarterly, 63*(4), 273–287. https://doi.org/10.1177/0016986219833738

Pfeiffer, S. I. (2012). Current perspectives on the identification and assessment of gifted students. *Journal of Psychoeducational Assessment, 30*(1), 3–9. https:// doi.org/10.1177/0734282911428192

Plucker, J. A., Burroughs, N., & Song, R. (2010). *Mind the (other) gap! The growing excellence gap in K–12 education.* Indiana University, Center for Evaluation and Education Policy.

Plucker, J. A., & Peters, S. J. (2016). *Excellence gaps in education: Expanding opportunities for talented students*. Harvard Education Press.

Rambo-Hernandez, K. E., Peters, S. J., & Plucker, J. A. (2019). Quantifying and exploring elementary school excellence gaps across schools and time. *Journal of Advanced Academics, 30*(4), 383–415. https://doi.org/10.1177/193220 2X19864116

Ritchhart, R., & Church, M. (2020). *The power of making thinking visible: Practices to engage and empower all learners*. Jossey-Bass.

Robinson, A., Adelson, J. L., Kidd, K. A., & Cunningham, C. M. (2018). A talent for tinkering: Developing talents in children from low-income households through engineering curriculum. *Gifted Child Quarterly, 62*(1) 130–144. https://doi.org/10.1177/0016986217738049

Rowland, A. (2016, April). *Design thinking: Catalyzing family engagement to support student learning*. https://archive.globalfrp.org/family-involvement/publi cations-resources/design-thinking-catalyzing-family-engagement-to-suppor t-student-learning

Sano, J. (2009). Farmhands and factory workers, honesty and humility: The portrayal of social class and morals in English language learner children's books. *Teachers College Record, 111*(11), 2560–2588.

Scott, M. S., Deuel, L.-L. S., Jean-Francois, B., & Urbano, R. C. (1996). Identifying cognitively gifted ethnic minority children. *Gifted Child Quarterly, 40*(3), 147–153. https://doi.org/10.1177/001698629604000305

Siegle, D. (2020, July). *Report from the National Center for Research on Gifted Education* [Presentation]. National Association for Gifted Children Leadership and Advocacy Conference. https://ncrge.uconn.edu/wp-content/uploads/sites/982/2020/11/2020_NAGC_Leadership_Conference_July_13_Siegle_Handout.pdf

Siegle, D., Gubbins, E. J., O'Rourke, P., Langley, S. D., Mun, R. U., Luria, S. R., Little, C. A., McCoach, B., Knupp, T., Callahan, C. M., & Plucker, J. A. (2016). Barriers to underserved students' participation in gifted programs and possible solutions. *Journal for the Education of the Gifted, 39*(2), 10–131. https://doi.org/10.1177/0162353216640930

Smith, J. R., Brooks-Gunn, J., & Klebanov, P. K. (1997). Consequences of living in poverty for young children's cognitive and verbal ability and early school achievement. In G. J. Duncan & J. Brooks-Gunn (Eds.), *Consequences of growing up poor* (pp. 132–138). Russell Sage Foundation.

Sotelo-Dynega, M., Ortiz, S. O., Flanagan, D. P., & Chaplin, W. F. (2013). English language proficiency and test performance: an evaluation of bilingual students with the Woodcock-Johnson III test of cognitive abilities. *Psychology in the Schools, 50*(8), 781–797. https://doi.org/10.1002/pits.21706

Speirs Neumeister, K. L., Adams, C. M., Pierce, R. L., Cassady, J. C., & Dixon, F. A. (2007) Fourth-grade teachers' perceptions of giftedness: Implications for identifying and serving diverse gifted students. *Journal for the Education of the Gifted, 30*(4), 479–499. https://doi.org/10.4219/jeg-2007-503

Swanson, J. D. (2006). Breaking through assumptions about low-income, minority gifted students. *Gifted Child Quarterly, 50*(1), 11–25. https://doi.org/10.1177/001698620605000103

Thadani, V., Cook, M. S., Griffis, K., Wise, J. A., & Blakey, A. (2010). The possibilities and limitations of curriculum-based science inquiry interventions for challenging the "pedagogy of poverty." *Equity & Excellence in Education, 43*(1), 21–37. https://doi.org/10.1080/10665680903408908

VanTassel-Baska, J. (1986). Effective curriculum and instruction models for the gifted. *Gifted Child Quarterly, 30*(4), 164–169. https://doi.org/10.1177/001698628603000404

VanTassel-Baska, J. (2017). Introduction to the Integrated Curriculum Model. In J. VanTassel-Baska & C. A. Little (Eds.). *Content-based curriculum for high-ability learners* (3rd ed., pp. 15–32). Prufrock Press.

VanTassel-Baska, J., Johnson, D., & Avery, L. D. (2002). Using performance tasks in the identification of economically disadvantaged and minority gifted learners: Findings from Project STAR. *Gifted Child Quarterly, 46*(2), 110–123. https://doi.org/10.1177/001698620204600204

VanTassel-Baska, J., & Little, C. A. (Eds.). (2017). *Content-based curriculum for high-ability learners* (3rd ed.). Prufrock Press.

VanTassel-Baska, J., & Stambaugh, T. (2006). *Comprehensive curriculum for gifted learners* (3rd ed.). Pearson.

VanTassel-Baska, J., & Stambaugh, T. (2020). *Affective Jacob's Ladder Reading Comprehension Program: Grade 3.* Prufrock Press.

Warshauer, H. K. (2015). Strategies to support productive struggle. *Mathematics Teaching in the Middle School, 20*(7), 390–393. https://doi.org/10.5951/mathteacmiddscho.20.7.0390

Wells, A. (2020). *Achieving equity in gifted programming: Dismantling barriers and tapping potential.* Prufrock Press.

Wolpert-Gawron, H. (2016). The many roles of an instructional coach. *Educational Leadership, 73*(9), 56–60. https://www.ascd.org/publications/educational-leadership/jun16/vol73/num09/The-Many-Roles-of-an-Instructional-Coach.aspx

Appendix

Sample Applications of Critical and Creative Thinking Strategies

The following examples expand on several of the strategies outlined in Chapter 3 (see Figures 6 and 7), providing some specific ways that teachers might employ the strategies and use questions to draw out student thinking.

Questioning

One important point to remember in focusing on questioning is to emphasize *student* questioning, not just teacher questioning. In approaching a new text, resource, problem, or other stimulus, questions such as these might be useful in encouraging students to ask questions:

- What more do we need to know?
- What do you wonder about our topic/idea?
- What problems or questions should we think about as our next step?
- What is a "why" question we could ask right now?
- Why is the topic important?
- What would you ask an expert about this?

Socratic Seminar

The Socratic seminar is one example of a thoughtful dialogue that fosters critical thinking, serves as a catalyst for lively discussions, and leads to a consideration of multiple viewpoints on issues, themes, and ideas. Named for the ancient Greek philosopher who believed that all knowledge is living and interactive, it is a method that teaches through questioning. Socrates believed that actively questioning another's ideas helps a person discover what they believe and the basis for their beliefs as well.

To begin a seminar discussion, the leader (adult or child) poses an open-ended question, such as "What is potential?" The first question may lead to other questions, such as "Does everyone have the same potential? What must you do to make sure that your potential is developed?" Participants share different viewpoints, support their opinions with clear reasoning and evidence, consider alternative views, and identify areas of agreement and disagreement. Through this dynamic discussion, children increase their understanding and expand their thinking in new and meaningful ways.

Classroom seminars may start out as open-ended questions; however, they may also be in response to a poem, news article, artwork, movie, or other piece of interest that would lead to a good discussion. After reading *My Great-Aunt Arizona* by Gloria Houston, a story about children who attended a one-room schoolhouse in the 1800s, students in one classroom discussed "What were the advantages and disadvantages of one-room schools?" Another class read the poem *The Road Not Taken* by Robert Frost. After sharing the poem, students discussed the importance of making thoughtful decisions and wondered, "Can you ever really know if you made the right decision as you go through life?"

The flow of ideas that the seminar fosters challenges students to question and defend their own thinking as they listen to others. It also provides students with practice in expressing and sharing their viewpoint with evidence from the text to support their thinking. Learning to examine various viewpoints increases students' willingness to consider the ideas of others and helps them understand that their own point of view may change as they listen to their peers. Gradually, with practice, they are able to listen to and learn from others, think critically about their own ideas, and identify areas of agreement and disagreement. Classroom discussions are raised to a new level when children are engaged in this strategy, and it provides teachers with an important opportunity to observe and record evidence of student thinking through oral expression.

Fluency, Originality, Flexibility, and Elaboration

There are many divergent thinking activities that encourage students in developing their ability to show fluency, originality, flexibility, and elaboration in their thinking. Some sample questions to prompt these skills include the following:

- How many ideas can you give in response to the question?
- What are some different approaches we could take to solving the problem or answering the question?
- Which of your ideas is the most unusual, and why?
- How can you explain your idea in more detail?
- Which of your classmates' ideas would you use? Why?
- (When creating categories) What can we add to category _____?
- What is another time you could use this strategy/solution?
- Which of the ideas is most efficient?

SCAMPER

Another approach that allows students to experience the power and application of critical and creative thinking is a creative brainstorming strategy called SCAMPER. The process of SCAMPER encourages children to think of new ideas, combine existing ideas in new ways, and generate original and often unusual ideas. Once they have opportunities to practice this type of thinking, students can improve their ability to make inventive or creative connections between ideas and also come up with new ideas. An important rule of brainstorming is that all ideas are accepted and none are judged. The process of suspending judgment is important as it emphasizes the need to accept all possibilities and helps to ensure and maintain an open mind. Many great inventions would have met an early end if the inventors had not been open to possibilities and continually thought of new ideas. Thomas Edison's light bulb is one such invention. Although other inventors had already invented an electric light bulb, the filaments that they used were not practical and either burnt out quickly or used too much electric current. Edison brainstormed with his team and conducted more than 1,200 experiments before finding a filament that would burn for a long time without burning out.

The originator of classical brainstorming was Alex Osborn. He formulated a checklist (Osborn, 1957) that could be used to transform an existing idea into a new one. His checklist was designed to have a flexible trial-and-error type of approach that could be used for thinking of and considering new ideas. Later, Bob Eberle (2008) took Osborn's checklist and developed SCAMPER, a process that allows children to brainstorm multiple possibilities and create unusual connections between objects, and/or ideas. SCAMPER is designed to encourage children to generate unique thoughts, explore relationships, and search for new or different combinations.

Each letter of the word SCAMPER is accompanied by questions and a thought process that encourages creative thinking.

Substitute. The S is for Substitute and is accompanied by questions such as, "What could you substitute? What might you do instead? What would work as well or better?" If you ask students to find examples of substitution in their everyday world, they will discover myriad inventions that have evolved from the idea of substitution. Scientists are continually brainstorming ideas and trying out new materials to improve efficiency (faster, lighter bicycles) or to make things safer (flame retardant material for pajamas).

Combine. The C is for Combine, and students are asked, "What could you combine? What might work well together? What could be brought together?" Many of the tools and appliances that we use each day are examples of ideas that have been combined: the clock radio, all of the capabilities of a cell phone, a pencil that converts to a pen, a watch with the calendar date, a printer that also serves as a copier and a scanner; the list is endless.

Adapt/Adjust. A is for Adapt or Adjust, in other words, changing something to fit a new situation. Questions that accompany this letter include, "What could be adjusted to suit a purpose or condition? How could you make it fit? Is there anything else like this?" One innovative designer is bringing the convenience of a vending machine to pedal-powered transportation and has adapted the concept of a vending machine to create fully automated rental units that hold up to 100 bicycles. Electric car companies adapted the use of the rechargeable battery to store and supply energy for motor vehicles. Another innovator adapted the common straw and created the "life straw" that filters polluted war and makes it safe to drink.

Modify/Magnify/Minify. M is for Modify, Magnify, or Minify. This one challenges children to think of ways to make something smaller or larger, or to change its color or shape. Questions might include, "Could you make it larger, greater, or stronger? Could you make it smaller, lighter, or slower? What would happen if you changed the color, sound, taste, or smell?" Children's books provide numerous examples of the results of this type of brainstorming. There are mini-books, books with cardboard pages for small children, "big books" for teachers to read aloud, books that readers can scratch and sniff and smell as the story is read, pop-up books, books with large print, and many others. The children's section of the library is a fun place to search for examples of modify, magnify, and minify.

Put to Other Uses. P stands for Put to Other Uses and asks children to think of how something could be used in another way. Questions include, "How could you use it for a different purpose? What are some new ways to apply it? Where else could you use it?" Planting seeds in an egg carton or hanging a tire from a tree for a swing are examples of how people put everyday objects to another use. In efforts to reduce waste, children are encouraged to think of other uses for items that otherwise would be discarded. Other examples may be found in the industrial world where cargo ships are now using kites and ropes to capture wind energy and reduce annual fuel costs.

Elimination. E is for Elimination or taking away a part of something in order to simplify it, or taking out unnecessary parts to reduce waste, cost, time, or effort. Questions that accompany this letter include, "What could you subtract or take away? What could you do without it?" Simplified packaging, online shopping, a cordless telephone, and organic foods without preservatives are just a few examples of how elimination has changed products and services.

Rearrange/Reverse. The final letter in SCAMPER is R, which stands for Rearrange or Reverse, or in other words, consider how to put things in a different order. Questions that lead to this type of thinking include, "What would you have if you reversed the order or turned it around? Could you change the parts, the layout, or the sequence?" Reversible clothes are an example of this concept that is very familiar to children. In addition, schedules are often rearranged to accommodate conflicting events. Fast food restaurants are examples of rearranging the order of service in a typical restaurant in order to save time. Instead of waiting for a server to take the order, customers pay first and are served second. Another example that would be familiar to children when playing music on an electronic device is the shuffle mode, which is a way to constantly rearrange the order in which the songs are played. Finally, *Choose Your Own Adventure* is a series of children's books in which the story and its outcome can be manipulated by the reader.

Once children become familiar with the letters and the thinking that they represent, you can send them on a SCAMPER scavenger hunt. The rules are simple: They can work alone or in teams, and they search for examples of SCAMPER in their room, their house, advertisements, or any other site—the world is full of examples!

SCAMPER Scavenger Hunt

Work in teams of two or more. Search for and locate the following:

❧ Something that can serve as a <u>substitute</u> for something else:

_____

❧ Something that has been <u>combined</u> for a new purpose:

_____

❧ Something that has been <u>adapted</u> for use:

_____

❧ Something that has been <u>modified</u> from nature:

_____

❧ What product was put to use in a way it was not intended?

_____

❧ What product represents an <u>elimination</u> for product improvement?

_____

❧ What is an example of <u>rearranged</u> parts?

_____

❧ What product was created from turning it upside down, backward, or inside out (<u>reverse</u>)?

_____

SCAMPER is a powerful tool that encourages fluid, flexible, and productive thinking through exercises that children can apply to their everyday world. It teaches them that many new ideas and inventions evolved from existing ideas and that as the world continues to evolve and change, people who have innovative ideas and solutions are needed more than ever. Once children become familiar with each letter and the thinking each represents, the possibilities for applications in their own lives and in their future work are endless. Application of the strategy gives teachers another opportunity to collect evidence of advanced potential as they find and nurture young scholars.

Visualization

Visualization provides opportunities for students to think about next steps, likely outcomes, and a variety of other projections. Visualization is also a useful tool for problem solving and for building self-efficacy, as students are encouraged to envision themselves succeeding. Here are some sample questions to encourage students in visualization:

- ❧ What do you think the next scene will look like? What will happen next?
- ❧ What will the pattern look like if we extend it?
- ❧ What can you see in your mind as possible next steps?
- ❧ If you visualize a change (e.g., changing a character, maybe to an animal with no thumbs), what would be the impact/outcome?
- ❧ If you were to change _____ (event, ending, what you visualized), how can you describe this new event/ending/etc.?
- ❧ What details can you change? How would the change in details change the big picture?

Mind Mapping

Mind mapping guides students to demonstrate their own understanding of how ideas and topics are connected. It is a useful and important strategy for developing understanding of patterns and connections, and a valuable assessment approach for teachers to gauge students' background and developing knowledge of a topic. Here are some example questions to prompt use of mind mapping:

- ❧ How could information on _____ be organized?
- ❧ What key _____ ideas can be used to create a mind map?
- ❧ What related details could be added to the mind map?
- ❧ How does the mind map summarize the topic?

Point of View

Understanding point of view is a central element of any critical thinking endeavor. Here are some sample questions for encouraging students to engage with point of view:

- ❧ Who are some of the people or groups who would be interested in this question or issue? What might they think about it and why?
- ❧ How might a different character describe the events of the story differently?
- ❧ What are some of the different paths that people might take to solve this problem?
- ❧ Who else should we ask for their perspective on the issue?

The Art of Persuasion

I Wanna Iguana by Karen Kaufman Orloff (2004) is the delightful story of a young boy's efforts to convince his mother to let him have an iguana that his best friend is giving away. Alex and his mother write back and forth a series of humorous notes and drawings that capture arguments he puts forth to persuade his mother to let him have an iguana for a pet. The book can serve as an excellent introduction to the art of persuasion. Persuasion is an important thinking skill, and as Alex learns in this story, it is one that can be learned through practice and reflection.

Persuasion is used quite broadly in today's society. Numerous advertisements promote their products on television, free samples are distributed through mail and in stores to entice buyers to try and then purchase products, and there are multiple venues for giving advice and suggesting what consumers should buy, how they should dress, what they should eat, where they should shop or travel, and the list goes on. Therefore, it is important for children to learn about persuasion and become aware of the techniques that are used to persuade others. For example, do Nike shoes really help people run faster? Or is it just the logo and branding that have made the company so successful? As students become adept at identifying how others persuade, their thinking and reflecting skills are strengthened through a continuous and critical examination of claims, ideas, questions, and research. They gradually learn to identify key aspects of a sound claim or argument and are better able to make decisions and/or persuade others based on sound reasoning and thinking.

More than 4,000 years ago, Aristotle identified four clusters of emotion and experiences that can be used to influence decisions or to persuade others. Aristotle believed that good people need to be aware of these four "appeals" so that they are able to use them to persuade others and to protect themselves from others who might try to persuade them. The four appeals are ethos (authority, expertise, or credibility), pathos (emotions), nomos (shared cultural connections and beliefs), and logos (logic, evidence or facts):

- **Ethos** is about trust. It appeals to the authority or credibility of the speaker or writer and is created through confidence in the knowledge, experiences, expertise, credentials, and/or professional standing of the speaker. A good example of ethos is when expert testimony is brought in to court and is used to persuade a jury. Teaching ethos to children helps them understand why they need to listen to the dentist (an expert who knows and understands what is necessary to have healthy teeth) or their pediatrician who tells them the importance of eating healthy foods. However, they should also be aware that ethos can be used to convince when there is no evidence to support the claim. In *I Wanna Iguana*, Alex's mother uses ethos to question Alex's credibility by bringing up a past experience when he brought home the class fish.

❧ **Pathos** is the art of appealing to another's emotions to persuade. It is used to attract an audience's sympathies and imagination. This occurs when guilt, love, security, greed, pity, humor, etc., are induced in the reader or listener. In *I Wanna Iguana*, Alex uses pathos in his first note when he tells his mom that if he doesn't take the iguana, it will go to Stinky, another friend, and his dog will eat it; Alex is hoping to elicit an emotional response to his plight. Images are especially effective in arousing emotions, and throughout the story, Alex and his mother use images and pictures to illustrate their opposing arguments. There are numerous examples of how images are used to elicit emotional reactions in the world today. For example, images of shrinking glaciers often accompany pleas to address global warming, and images of kittens and puppies accompany information about animal adoptions. As children become aware of pathos and are able to identify examples of it in everyday life, they are better prepared to recognize its use and understand its role in persuasion.

❧ **Nomos** is using shared cultural beliefs to persuade. It is invoked by pointing out what the parties have in common and expanding upon the similarities. Peer pressure is a form of nomos, and children are often subject to persuasion because they want to belong to a certain group. This can be a positive experience, such as Boy Scouts and Girl Scouts, a swim team, or a youth group; however, it can also be negative, such as gangs and cliques. It is important for children to understand and reflect on the reasons they are joining a group. These reasons should go beyond a need to belong or a need for approval. From youth activities to peer groups to school pride, nomos can be used as a positive or negative force to persuade others to join, participate, or act a certain way.

❧ **Logos** is employing logic, providing facts, or sharing evidence that most will agree is "real." Logos may take the form of details, facts, statistics, and other information that has some form of empirical evidence to support its claim. In *I Wanna Iguana*, Alex uses logos when he states that iguanas are quiet and small. His mom replies with logos when she tells him that they can grow to be more than 6 feet long! Fact checking is a critical component of logos. Two questions that can guide children's thinking about logos are: *From whose viewpoint are we seeing or reading or hearing? What is the evidence, and how reliable is it?*

Students can become familiar with each of the appeals by finding, identifying, and discussing numerous examples in their everyday lives. Magazines and commercials are filled with illustrations of how the different appeals are used to persuade others. As a class, you may want to collect examples of the different appeals over time. Reflect on and discuss these questions: *Which ads have persuaded you or someone you know to try an item? What impacted your decision? Would you make a different decision now?*

Gradually children learn that all of the appeals are important and interdependent. To win a good argument, they must be credible, well-informed, and have research-based knowledge of the topic, claim, or issue. Although stories, images, and pictures can elicit emotions in order to persuade others, they are not enough; more information and evidence are needed. Shared beliefs and common points of interest can be powerful tools of persuasion, as they appeal to a need to belong; however, they also require a critical review of reasons why one particular group should be chosen rather than or in addition to another. And finally, facts, statistics, and empirical evidence are critical. If a claim is made, evidence must be provided, and this may be the most important lesson of all.

As students practice the art of formulating and designing convincing arguments with evidence to support their thinking, the art of persuasion can be a powerful tool that will help them navigate the many forms of persuasion that are part of their everyday lives. It also gives teachers an important opportunity to gather evidence of students who demonstrate more advanced applications of this thinking.

de Bono's Thinking Hats

Another strategy that promotes the consideration of multiple viewpoints is Edward de Bono's (1985) *Six Thinking Hats*. This thinking strategy provides a colorful structure to guide students in the discussion of a topic or issue from six different perspectives. There are six colored hats, and each color represents a different type of thinking. The white hat is used for facts and evidence, the red hat elicits feelings or emotions that are associated with the topic, the yellow hat focuses on the positive aspects, and the black hat focuses on the negative aspects. The green hat encourages creativity as students formulate new ideas and solutions that may not have been considered initially. Finally, the blue hat helps them organize their thinking and design a plan to move forward. The colors provide an important visual that children associate with each type of thinking as they use it to solve problems, address issues, or make decisions. Each hat is equal in value and helps students focus on one type of thinking at a time. As children learn how to talk about each hat and the associated thinking, they begin to realize the difference between facts and emotions and how one can influence the other. They realize the importance of considering both the positive and negative aspects of an idea. The six colors and the type of thinking that accompany each one raises student awareness of the complexity of the thinking process.

Analogies

Analogies help students to build connections and recognize patterns and relationships. Here are some sample questions for supporting students' use of analogies:

- ❧ How is a _____ like a _____?
- ❧ How would _____ feel if _____ were a _____?
- ❧ If _____ were a _____, what would _____ see, feel, and think?
- ❧ In what ways is a _____ like a _____?

There are three kinds of analogy that may be used to stretch and extend children's thinking, and each one becomes more complex as it is applied.

Direct Analogy

The first, the direct analogy, is a lot of fun and a good place to begin. *My Best Friend Is as Sharp as a Pencil* is a lighthearted picture book in which a child describes her teachers and friends by comparing them to common objects. For example, one friend is quiet like a fish and another is clever like LEGO. Through the use of analogies, the author has the child create a portrait of her school day that is creative, humorous, and engaging to readers. It may be important to note that simple analogies are different from similes because their purpose is to find an unexpected similarity between unrelated things rather than just comparing two things. After reading the book, you may ask your students to describe their own friends using comparisons. When asked to do this, one young boy replied that his friend is "like a monkey because he is silly but also like a tornado because he has strong opinions." Another young girl who was asked to use direct analogies to describe her dog said, "her fur is like a carpet when I pet her because she is so soft, and her ears are like leaves because they flap in the wind." Picture books are fun to read and provide practice in understanding and applying analogies. *Animalogy: Animal Analogies* by Marianne Berkes is a fun rhyming book that compares and contrasts very different animals by pointing out their similarities. Once children understand how analogies work, there are numerous questions and sentence starters that may be used to stimulate the imagination and lead them to deeper understandings by connecting things that do not always appear connected. Examples include:

- Which flower is most like you? Explain.
- Books are like musical instruments because . . .
- How is a friendship like an ocean?
- How is solving a problem like riding a bike?

Another way of working with analogies is the use of pictures to stimulate creative thinking and expression. For example, you can spread photographs from old calendars and magazines on a table and ask a child to choose pictures that best describe them and ask them to explain why. One teacher did this with her students and asked each one to select a picture that described them as a learner. One student picked a flower and said, "The flower shows how I learn because I learn little by little and so bud by bud." Another child chose a city because "when I am thinking about something, a lot goes on in my head, just like a city," and another chose dominoes falling because "I have to make mistakes a lot of times before I reach the end. The dominoes also are like when I fall down I have to pick myself up again."

Personal Analogy

The second type of analogy is the personal analogy. This type of thinking challenges children to become the object of comparison and includes questions such as "How does it feel to be a volcano, a LEGO, or a snowstorm?" The focus is on feelings and giving children an opportunity to empathize with the object, become personally involved, and express different feelings. Students are asked how it would feel to be the object and why. For example, one child was asked, "How does it feel to be a LEGO?" Responses included:

- creative because I am part of a structure,
- insignificant because no one notices me by myself,
- crowded because I am in a pile with a bunch of different LEGO,
- colorful like a rainbow,
- lonely when I am stored,

- excited because somebody might build something with me,
- suspended because people might stack me or leave me somewhere,
- important because every part is needed, and
- trapped because I am connected to other LEGO.

Symbolic Analogy

The third analogy, the symbolic analogy, is more complex and builds on the thinking of the first two types of analogy, the direct and the personal. It is created by asking a student to put together opposite feelings that were listed in the personal analogy that seem to conflict or are charged with tension. Together these feelings create an oxymoron and stimulate creative thinking. For example, in the responses about how it feels to be a LEGO, a child might put together Insignificant/Important, Creative/Crowded, Excited/Lonely, or Suspended/Trapped. The symbolic analogy is created by asking children to think of an object that captures one pair of feelings. For example, one child said that a "bicycle is excited and lonely—excited when it is out exploring the world and lonely when it is put away waiting to be ridden." Another said that a "ceiling fan is excited when it is spinning around and lonely when it is turned off because it just hangs from the ceiling." The final step in the symbolic analogy is to ask a child to compare the object associated with the paired feelings to a topic or concept. For example, you might ask, "How is thinking like a bicycle?" One child responded,

> Thinking is exciting because the ideas go around and around, they are both useful, a bicycle has different gears and there are different types of thinking, sometimes a bike goes fast and sometimes slow and same with thinking, someone can help you ride your bike and someone can help you be a better thinker, sometimes you ride with others and sometimes you ride alone and thinking is the same. They are both fun!

Analogies help students see relationships and connections among objects and ideas in an original light. Creating and connecting with analogies enhances flexible thinking and helps students see the world in new and unusual ways. New ideas emerge, and new approaches to solving a problem may surface; the possibilities are endless. The power of analogies to capture and stimulate the imagination of a child should never be underestimated.

Encapsulation

Encapsulation focuses on encouraging students to get to the heart or the central understanding of what they are studying and communicating. Here are some sample questions that will help with engaging students with encapsulation:

- ❧ In one sentence, what is the most important understanding to take away from our activity today?
- ❧ If you were to write a headline for what we learned about today, what would the headline be?
- ❧ What hashtag or meme would you use to capture what we learned about today?
- ❧ What is the most essential thing to remember about our topic today?
- ❧ How might you use a visual representation to capture what we talked about today?
- ❧ You have 10 words to represent what we learned today—you can use sentences or phrases but should use 10 (or 5!) total words.
- ❧ Can you write a tweet explaining the main idea of what we learned today?
- ❧ What was the most important thing we learned today?

Decisions and Outcomes

Many instructional activities can provide the context for students to explore decisions and outcomes. Here are some sample questions for prompting attention to this strategy:

- ❧ What were/are the options for the decision to be made? What are the likely outcomes for each option?
- ❧ What information was/is needed for making the decision?
- ❧ What consequences resulted from a decision?
- ❧ When making a decision, what kinds of things may influence which option we choose?

Decisions, Decisions, Decisions . . . and Outcomes

"You can't judge a book by its cover" is an age-old adage that lies at the heart of this decision-making strategy. The next time you browse through a bookstore, take a look at the creativity and color that goes into designing a book cover as publishers compete to capture the reader's attention and sell their product. Everyone has selected books at one time or another based on superficial reasoning; sometimes the selection truly is a great book, and other times it is a disappointment. Book selection is just one of many choices children make each school day as they practice making decisions and dealing with the outcomes.

With practice, children can learn to assess and evaluate a variety of decisions and possible outcomes. This helps them understand the importance of examining multiple outcomes before embarking on a course of action. The concept of examining outcomes is relevant for all students as they learn to consider both short-term and long-term consequences in the decision-making process.

A simple T-chart can be used to set up the decision making process. For example:

Decision: Should I play afterschool soccer?

Short-Term Outcomes	Long-Term Outcomes
➽ Less time to play after school	➽ I may learn to manage my time
➽ I may not be on a team with my best friend	better
➽ Soccer requires practice and hard work	➽ I may make new friends
➽ I will get a uniform, shin guards, and cool shoes	➽ I will build up endurance and speed
	➽ I will learn new skills

Over time students begin to see a pattern in the decision-making process and find that often the long-term outcomes are the opposite of the short term. For example, a decision about whether or not to do homework may yield the short-term outcome of more free time to play; however, the long-term outcome might be that the student has to stay after school another day to complete missed assignments, which ultimately negates the short-term outcome of more time to play.

As children get older they can learn the value of research and how to use information to make decisions. Consumer guides, ratings and reviews, and questioning experts are just a few of the resources that are readily available to inform decision making with guidance. For example, if a child is interested in purchasing an electronic device, a helpful strategy would be learning to review and compare different makes, brands, and/or features in a consumer guide, either online or offline. Book reviews are also available online, and children can take time to read what others think of a book. They can also learn to write and add their own book review. Interviews with experts also provide valuable information. If a child is deciding whether or not to play a certain instrument, they may want to interview a professional who plays that instrument to learn about the practice, training, and techniques that are part of a journey toward expertise. Whether it is a product or a service, it is always important to read and learn not only what the positive reviewers have to say, but the negative aspects as well. Over time, children learn the importance of an informed decision-making process.

A focus on decisions and outcomes also has broad applications to subjects taught in school, and these subjects can be used to deepen students' understanding of decision making. History is replete with examples of leaders and nations that made decisions with serious implications for the world. For example, the colonists made a decision to revolt against British tyranny, which led to the American Revolution (Loyalists made a decision to remain loyal to the king of England, and consequently many returned to England), President Abraham Lincoln issued the Emancipation Proclamation, which had critical short-term (freedom for thousands of slaves) and long-term consequences (the Thirteenth Amendment of the Constitution of the United States, which guaranteed the permanent abolition of slavery).

Literature is another excellent source of examples of decisions made and the outcomes that characters in stories and novels face as a result of their decisions. In the story of the Three Little Pigs, each pig had to deal with the consequences of the decision he made on which material to use to build his home. The first pig, who made his home of straw, had more time to play in the short term; however, in the long term he lost his home completely and had to move in with his wiser brother! In fictional writing, students have an opportunity to think about the decisions that authors make as they write each story, knowing that each decision will lead to an outcome that will impact the plot and the story's end. Mathematicians and scientists continually make decisions and review the outcomes of their decisions based on evidence that is a result of the decision-making process. New discoveries in mathematics and science are based on the work of experts in the field making decisions, evaluating outcomes, and seeking to learn more in a wide variety of specialized areas. In all of these examples, the decisions made and the consequences of those decisions (both long and short term) help students gain a much deeper understanding of the importance of those decisions and their impact on the world.

Decision making is integral to everything students do. Helping children learn and understand the thinking processes that lead to good decisions is an important skill that will serve them well now and in the future. It is another powerful way of gathering evidence of students with the potential to apply this thinking in ways that are advanced in comparison to their peers.

Plus, Minus, Interesting (PMI)

PMI supports students in considering a variety of perspectives and outcomes about a topic or situation. Some guiding questions are as follows:

- ❧ What are the +, −, and interesting ideas about_____?
- ❧ What is the value of _____?
- ❧ What would most people not know about _____?
- ❧ What would happen to your responses if you substituted modify for minus?

About the Authors

Carol V. Horn, Ed.D., has worked extensively to develop and implement the Young Scholars Model, a comprehensive approach to finding and developing talent and gifted potential in young learners from underrepresented populations. Carol was coordinator of Advanced Academic Programs for Fairfax County Public Schools (FCPS) for 17 years and has worked in gifted education for more than 30 years. She is a National Board Certified Teacher and past president of the Virginia Association for the Gifted. She has a master's in education in educational psychology with an emphasis on gifted from the University of Virginia and a doctorate in teacher preparation and special education from The George Washington University.

Catherine A. Little, Ph.D., is a Professor in Giftedness, Creativity, and Talent Development in the Department of Educational Psychology at the University of Connecticut. She earned her Ph.D. in Educational Policy, Planning, and Administration with emphasis on Gifted Education Administration from William & Mary. Her research interests include professional learning, differentiation of curriculum and instruction, and classroom ques-

209

tioning practices. Recently, she has been project director for Project SPARK and Project LIFT, both of which are federally funded research initiatives focused on working with schools and teachers to recognize and respond to advanced academic potential in the early grades, particularly in students from underserved populations.

Kirsten Maloney has worked in gifted education for more than 15 years in a variety of roles, including central office, elementary Advanced Academic Resource Teacher, Young Scholars lead teacher and curriculum writer, and gifted and general education classroom teacher. She is currently the K–12 Coordinator of Advanced Academic Programs (AAP) in Fairfax County Public Schools in Northern Virginia. Kirsten is a National Board Certified Teacher, has a master's in educational psychology with an emphasis in gifted education from the University of Virginia and certification in educational leadership from The George Washington University, and is currently an Ed.D. student in educational leadership at the University of Virginia.

Cheryl McCullough is currently working as the K–12 Supervisor for Gifted Services in Arlington Public Schools in Arlington, VA. She has worked in gifted education for 30 years in a variety of roles, including gifted specialist, gifted center teacher, Schoolwide Enrichment Model (SEM) specialist, and curriculum writer. She worked in the AAP office in Fairfax County Public Schools and worked with a team to support the Young Scholars Model. She initiated the Young Scholars Model in Arlington Public Schools. Cheryl served as a board member for the National Association for the Gifted (NAGC), is a past president of Virginia Association for the Gifted, earned her National Board Certification, and was awarded the Mover and Shaker Award from Future Problem Solving of Virginia. She has an Ed.S. in administration and supervision, an M.A. in curriculum and instruction, and a B.A. in political science, all three earned from Virginia Tech.